Thoughts out of Season

Part I

Friedrich Wilhelm Nietzsche

Alpha Editions

This edition published in 2023

ISBN : 9789357947145

Design and Setting By
Alpha Editions
www.alphaedis.com
Email - info@alphaedis.com

EDITORIAL NOTE.

THE Editor begs to call attention to some of the difficulties he had to encounter in preparing this edition of the complete works of Friedrich Nietzsche. Not being English himself, he had to rely upon the help of collaborators, who were somewhat slow in coming forward. They were also few in number; for, in addition to an exact knowledge of the German language, there was also required sympathy and a certain enthusiasm for the startling ideas of the original, as well as a considerable feeling for poetry, and that highest form of it, religious poetry.

Such a combination—a biblical mind, yet one open to new thoughts—was not easily found. And yet it was necessary to find translators with such a mind, and not be satisfied, as the French are and must be, with a free though elegant version of Nietzsche. What is impossible and unnecessary in French—a faithful and powerful rendering of the psalmistic grandeur of Nietzsche —is possible and necessary in English, which is a rougher tongue of the Teutonic stamp, and moreover, like German, a tongue influenced and formed by an excellent version of the Bible. The English would never be satisfied, as Bible-ignorant France is, with a Nietzsche *à l'Eau de Cologne*— they would require the natural, strong, real Teacher, and would prefer his outspoken words to the finely-chiselled sentences of the *raconteur*. It may indeed be safely predicted that once the English people have recovered from the first shock of Nietzsche's thoughts, their biblical training will enable them, more than any other nation, to appreciate the deep piety underlying Nietzsche's Cause.

As this Cause is a somewhat holy one to the Editor himself, he is ready to listen to any suggestions as to improvements of style or sense coming from qualified sources. The Editor, during a recent visit to Mrs. Foerster-Nietzsche at Weimar, acquired the rights of translation by pointing out to her that in this way her brother's works would not fall into the hands of an ordinary publisher and his staff of translators: he has not, therefore, entered into any engagement with publishers, not even with the present one, which could hinder his task, bind him down to any text found faulty, or make him consent to omissions or the falsification or "sugaring" of the original text to further the sale of the books. He is therefore in a position to give every attention to a work which he considers as of no less importance for the country of his residence than for the country of his birth, as well as for the rest of Europe.

It is the consciousness of the importance of this work which makes the Editor anxious to point out several difficulties to the younger student of Nietzsche. The first is, of course, not to begin reading Nietzsche at too early an age. While fully admitting that others may be more gifted than himself, the Editor begs to state that he began to study Nietzsche at the age of twenty-six, and would not have been able to endure the weight of such teaching before that time. Secondly, the Editor wishes to dissuade the student from beginning the study of Nietzsche by reading first of all his most complicated works. Not having been properly prepared for them, he will find the *Zarathustra* abstruse, the *Ecce Homo* conceited, and the *Antichrist* violent. He should rather begin with the little pamphlet on Education, the *Thoughts out of Season, Beyond Good and Evil*, or the *Genealogy of Morals*. Thirdly, the Editor wishes to remind students of Nietzsche's own advice to them, namely: to read him slowly, to think over what they have read, and not to accept too readily a teaching which they have only half understood. By a too ready acceptance of Nietzsche it has come to pass that his enemies are, as a rule, a far superior body of men to those who call themselves his eager and enthusiastic followers. Surely it is not every one who is chosen to combat a religion or a morality of two thousand years' standing, first within and then without himself; and whoever feels inclined to do so ought at least to allow his attention to be drawn to the magnitude of his task.

NIETZSCHE IN ENGLAND:

AN INTRODUCTORY ESSAY BY THE EDITOR.

DEAR ENGLISHMEN,—In one of my former writings I have made the remark that the world would have seen neither the great Jewish prophets nor the great German thinkers, if the people from among whom these eminent men sprang had not been on the whole such a misguided, and, in their misguidedness, such a tough and stubborn race. The arrow that is to fly far must be discharged from a well distended bow: if, therefore, anything is necessary for greatness, it is a fierce and tenacious opposition, an opposition either of open contempt, or of malicious irony, or of sly silence, or of gross stupidity, an opposition regardless of the wounds it inflicts and of the precious lives it sacrifices, an opposition that nobody would dare to attack who was not prepared, like the Spartan of old, to return either with his shield or on it.

An opposition so devoid of pity is not as a rule found amongst you, dear and fair-minded Englishmen, which may account for the fact that you have neither produced the greatest prophets nor the greatest thinkers in this world. You would never have crucified Christ, as did the Jews, or driven Nietzsche into madness, as did the Germans—you would have made Nietzsche, on account of his literary faculties, Minister of State in a Whig Ministry, you would have invited Jesus Christ to your country houses, where he would have been worshipped by all the ladies on account of his long hair and interesting looks, and tolerated by all men as an amusing, if somewhat romantic, foreigner. I know that the current opinion is to the contrary, and that your country is constantly accused, even by yourselves, of its insularity; but I, for my part, have found an almost feminine receptivity amongst you in my endeavour to bring you into contact with some ideas of my native country—a receptivity which, however, has also this in common with that of the female mind, that evidently nothing sticks deeply, but is quickly wiped out by what any other lecturer, or writer, or politician has to tell you. I was prepared for indifference—I was not prepared for receptivity and that benign lady's smile, behind which ladies, like all people who are only clever, usually hide their inward contempt for the foolishness of mere men! I was prepared for abuse, and even a good fight—I was not prepared for an extremely faint-hearted criticism; I did not expect that some of my opponents would be so utterly inexperienced in that most necessary work of literary execution. No, no: give me the Germans or the Jews for executioners: they can do the hanging properly, while the English hangman is like the Russian, to whom, when the rope broke, the half-hanged revolutionary said: "What a country, where they cannot hang a man properly!" What a country, where they do not hang philosophers properly—which would be the proper thing to do to them—but smile at them, drink tea with them, discuss with them, and ask them to contribute to their newspapers!

To get to the root of the matter: in spite of many encouraging signs, remarks and criticisms, adverse or benevolent, I do not think I have been very successful in my crusade for that European thought which began with Goethe and has found so fine a development in Nietzsche. True, I have made many a convert, but amongst them are very undesirable ones, as, for instance, some enterprising publishers, who used to be the toughest disbelievers in England, but who have now come to understand the "value" of the new gospel—but as neither this gospel is exactly Christian, nor I, the importer of it, I am not allowed to count my success by the conversion of publishers and sinners, but have to judge it by the more spiritual standard of the quality of the converted. In this respect, I am sorry to say, my success has been a very poor one.

As an eager missionary, I have naturally asked myself the reason of my failure. Why is there no male audience in England willing to listen to a manly and daring philosophy? Why are there no eyes to see, no ears to hear, no hearts to feel, no brains to understand? Why is my trumpet, which after all I know how to blow pretty well, unable to shatter the walls of English prejudice against a teacher whose school cannot possibly be avoided by any European with a higher purpose in his breast?... There is plenty of time for thought nowadays for a man who does not allow himself to be drawn into that aimless bustle of pleasure business or politics, which is called modern life because outside that life there is—just as outside those noisy Oriental cities-a desert, a calmness, a true and almost majestic leisure, a leisure unprecedented in any age, a leisure in which one may arrive at several conclusions concerning English indifference towards the new thought.

First of all, of course, there stands in the way the terrible abuse which Nietzsche has poured upon the heads of the innocent Britishers. While France and the Latin countries, while the Orient and India, are within the range of his sympathies, this most outspoken of all philosophers, this prophet and poet-philosopher, cannot find words enough to express his disgust at the illogical, plebeian, shallow, utilitarian Englishman. It must certainly be disagreeable to be treated like this, especially when one has a fairly good opinion of one's self; but why do you take it so very, very seriously? Did Nietzsche, perchance, spare the Germans? And aren't you accustomed to criticism on the part of German philosophers? Is it not the ancient and time-honoured privilege of the whole range of them from Leibnitz to Hegel — even of German poets, like Goethe and Heine — to call you bad names and to use unkind language towards you? Has there not always been among the few thinking heads in Germany a silent consent and an open contempt for you and your ways; the sort of contempt you yourselves have for the even more Anglo-Saxon culture of the Americans? I candidly confess that in my more German moments I have felt and still feel as the German philosophers do; but I have also my European turns and moods, and then I try to understand you and even excuse you, and take your part against earnest and thinking Germany. Then I feel like telling the German philosophers that if you, poor fellows, had practised everything they preached, they would have had to renounce the pleasure of abusing you long ago, for there would now be no more Englishmen left to abuse! As it is, you have suffered enough on account of the wild German ideals you luckily only partly believed in: for what the German thinker wrote on patient paper in his study, you always had to write the whole world over on tender human skins, black and yellow skins, enveloping ungrateful beings who sometimes had no very high esteem for the depth and beauty of German philosophy. And you have never taken revenge upon the inspired masters of the European thinking-shop, you have never reabused them, you have never complained of their want of worldly wisdom: you have invariably suffered in silence and agony, just as brave and staunch Sancho Panza used to do. For this is what you are, dear Englishmen, and however well you brave, practical, materialistic John Bulls and Sancho Panzas may know this world, however much better you may be able to perceive, to count, to judge, and to weigh things than your ideal German Knight: there is an eternal law in this world that the Sancho Panzas have to follow the Don Quixotes; for matter has to follow the spirit, even the poor spirit of a German philosopher! So it has been in the past, so it is at present, and so it will be in the future; and you had better prepare yourselves in time for the eventuality. For if Nietzsche were nothing else but this customary type of German philosopher, you would again have to pay the bill largely; and it would be very wise on your part to study him: Sancho Panza may escape a good many sad experiences by knowing his master's weaknesses. But as Nietzsche no longer belongs to the Quixotic class, as Germany seems to emerge with him from her youthful and cranky nebulosity, you will not even have the pleasure of being thrashed in the company of your Master: no, you will be thrashed all alone, which is an abominable thing for any right-minded human being. "Solamen miseris socios habuisse malorum."*

[Footnote * : It is a comfort to the afflicted to have companions in their distress.]

The second reason for the neglect of Nietzsche in this country is that you do not need him yet. And you do not need him yet because you have always possessed the British virtue of not carrying things to extremes, which, according to the German version, is an euphemism for the British want of logic and critical capacity. You have, for instance, never let your religion have any great influence upon your politics, which is something quite abhorrent to the moral German, and makes him so angry about you. For the German sees you acting as a moral and law-abiding Christian at home, and as an unscrupulous and Machiavellian conqueror abroad; and if he refrains from the reproach of hypocrisy, with which the more stupid continentals invariably charge you, he will certainly call you a "British muddlehead." Well, I myself do not take things so seriously as that, for I know that men of action have seldom time to think. It is probably for this reason also that liberty of thought and speech has been granted to you, the law-giver knowing very well all the time that you would be much too busy to use and abuse such extraordinary freedom. Anyhow, it might now be time to abuse it just a little bit, and to consider what an extraordinary amalgamation is a Christian Power with imperialistic ideas. True, there has once before been another Christian conquering and colonising empire like yours, that of Venice—but these Venetians were thinkers compared with you, and smuggled their gospel into the paw of their lion.... Why don't you follow their example, in order not to be unnecessarily embarrassed by it in your enterprises abroad? In this manner you could also reconcile the proper Germans, who invariably act up to their theories, their Christianity, their democratic principles, although, on the other hand, in so doing you would, I quite agree, be most unfaithful to your own traditions, which are of a more democratic character than those of any other European nation.

For Democracy, as every schoolboy knows, was born in an English cradle: individual liberty, parliamentary institutions, the sovereign rights of the people, are ideas of British origin, and have been propagated from this island over the whole of Europe. But as the prophet and his words are very often not honoured in his own country, those ideas have been embraced with much more fervour by other nations than by that in which they originated. The Continent of Europe has taken the desire for liberty and equality much more seriously than their levelling but also level-headed inventors, and the fervent imagination of France has tried to put into practice all that was quite hidden to the more sober English eye. Every one nowadays knows the good and the evil consequences of the French Revolution, which swept over the whole of Europe, throwing it into a state of unrest, shattering thrones and empires, and everywhere undermining authority and traditional institutions. While this was going on in Europe, the originator of the merry game was quietly sitting upon his island smiling broadly at the excitable foreigners across the Channel, fishing as much as he could out of the water he himself had so cleverly disturbed, and thus in every way reaping the benefit from the mighty fight for the apple of Eros which he himself had thrown amongst them. As I have endeavoured above to draw a parallel between the Germans and the Jews, I may now be allowed to follow this up with one between the Jews and the English. It is a striking parallel, which will specially appeal to those religious souls amongst you who consider themselves the lost tribes of our race (and who are perhaps even more lost than they think),—and it is this: Just as the Jews have brought Christianity into the world, but never accepted it themselves, just as they, in spite of their *democratic offspring*, have always remained the most conservative, exclusive, aristocratic, and religious people, so have the English never allowed themselves to be intoxicated by the strong drink of the natural equality of men, which they once kindly offered to all Europe to quaff; but have, on the contrary, remained the most sober, the most exclusive, the most feudal, the most conservative people of our continent.

But because the ravages of Democracy have been less felt here than abroad, because there is a good deal of the mediaeval building left standing over here, because things have never been carried to that excess which invariably brings a reaction with it—this reaction has not set in in this country, and no strong desire for the necessity of it, no craving for the counterbalancing influence of a Nietzsche, has arisen yet in the British mind. I cannot help pointing out the grave consequences of this backwardness of England, which has arisen from the fact that you have never taken any ideas or theories, not even your own, seriously. Democracy, dear Englishmen, is like a stream, which all the peoples of Europe will have to cross: they will come out of it cleaner, healthier, and stronger, but while the others are already in the water, plunging, puffing, paddling, losing their ground, trying to swim, and even half-drowned, you are still standing on the other side of it, roaring unmercifully about the poor swimmers, screamers, and fighters below,—but one day you will have to cross this same river too, and when you enter it the others will just be out of it, and will laugh at the poor English straggler in their turn!

The third and last reason for the icy silence which has greeted Nietzsche in this country is due to the fact that he has—as far as I know—no literary ancestor over here whose teachings could have prepared you for him. Germany has had her Goethe to do this; France her Stendhal; in Russia we find that fearless curiosity for all problems, which is the sign of a youthful, perhaps too youthful nation; while in Spain, on the other hand, we have an old and experienced people, with a long training away from Christianity under the dominion of the Semitic Arabs, who undoubtedly left some of their blood behind,—but I find great difficulty in pointing out any man over here who could serve as a useful guide to the heights of the Nietzschean thought, except one, who was not a Britisher. I am alluding to a man whose politics you used to consider and whose writings you even now consider as fantastic, but who, like another fantast of his race, may possess the wonderful gift of resurrection, and come again to life amongst you—to Benjamin Disraeli.

The Disraelian Novels are in my opinion the best and only preparation for those amongst you who wish gradually to become acquainted with the Nietzschean spirit. There, and nowhere else, will you find the true heroes of coming times, men of moral courage, men whose failures and successes are alike admirable, men whose noble passions have altogether superseded the ordinary vulgarities and moralities of lower beings, men endowed with an extraordinary imagination, which, however, is balanced by an equal power of reason, men already anointed with a drop of that sacred and noble oil, without which the High Priest-Philosopher of Modern Germany would not have crowned his Royal Race of the Future.

Both Disraeli and Nietzsche you perceive starting from the same pessimistic diagnosis of the wild anarchy, the growing melancholy, the threatening Nihilism of Modern Europe, for both recognised the danger of the age behind its loud and forced "shipwreck gaiety," behind its big-mouthed talk about progress and evolution, behind that veil of business-bustle, which hides its fear and utter despair—but for all that black outlook they are not weaklings enough to mourn and let things go, nor do they belong to that cheap class of society doctors who mistake the present wretchedness of Humanity for sinfulness, and wish to make their patient less sinful and still more wretched. Both Nietzsche and Disraeli have clearly recognised that this patient of theirs is suffering from weakness and not from sinfulness, for which latter some kind of strength may still be required; both are therefore entirely opposed to a further dieting him down to complete moral emaciation, but are, on the contrary, prescribing a tonic, a roborating, a natural regime for him —advice for which both doctors have been reproached with Immorality by their contemporaries as well as by posterity. But the younger doctor has turned the tables upon their accusers, and has openly reproached his Nazarene colleagues with the Immorality of endangering life itself, he has clearly demonstrated to the world that their trustful and believing patient was shrinking beneath their very fingers, he has candidly foretold these Christian quacks that one day they would be in the position of the quack skin-specialist at the fair, who, as a proof of his medical skill, used to show to the peasants around him the skin of a completely cured patient of his. Both Nietzsche and Disraeli know the way to health, for they have had the disease of the age themselves, but they have—the one partly, the other entirely— cured themselves of it, they have resisted the spirit of their time, they have escaped the fate of their contemporaries; they therefore, and they alone, know their danger. This is the reason why they both speak so violently, why they both attack with such bitter fervour the utilitarian and materialistic attitude of English Science, why they both so ironically brush aside the airy and fantastic ideals of German Philosophy—this is why they both loudly declare (to use Disraeli's words) "that we are the slaves of false knowledge; that our memories are filled with ideas that have no origin in truth; that we believe what our fathers credited, who were convinced without a cause; that we study human nature in a charnel house, and, like the nations of the East, pay divine honours to the maniac and the fool." But if these two great men cannot refrain from such outspoken vituperation—they also lead the way: they both teach the divinity of ideas and the vileness of action without principle; they both exalt the value of personality and character; they both deprecate the influence of society and socialisation; they both intensely praise and love life, but they both pour contempt and irony upon the shallow optimist, who thinks it delightful, and the quietist, who wishes it to be calm, sweet, and peaceful. They thus both preach a life of danger, in opposition to that of pleasure, of comfort, of happiness, and they do not only preach this noble life, they also act it: for both have with equal determination staked even their lives on the fulfilment of their ideal.

It is astonishing—but only astonishing to your superficial student of the Jewish character—that in Disraeli also we find an almost Nietzschean appreciation of that eternal foe of the Jewish race, the Hellenist, which makes Disraeli, just like Nietzsche, confess that the Greek and the Hebrew are both amongst the highest types of the human kind. It is not less astonishing—but likewise easily intelligible for one who knows something of the great Jews of the Middle Ages—that in Disraeli we discover that furious enmity against the doctrine of the natural equality of men which Nietzsche combated all his life. It was certainly the great Maimonides himself, that spiritual father of Spinoza, who guided the pen of his Sephardic descendant, when he thus wrote in his *Tancred*: "It is to be noted, although the Omnipotent Creator might have formed, had it pleased him, in the humblest of his creations, an efficient agent for his purpose that Divine Majesty has never thought fit to communicate except with human beings of the very highest order."

But what about Christianity, to which Disraeli was sincerely attached, and whose creation he always considered as one of the eternal glories of his race? Did not the Divine Majesty think it fit then to communicate with the most humble of its creatures, with the fishermen of Galilee, with the rabble of Corinth, with the slaves, the women, the criminals of the Roman Empire? As I wish to be honest about Disraeli, I must point out here, that his genius, although the most prominent in England during his lifetime, and although violently opposed to its current superstitions, still partly belongs to his age— and for this very pardonable reason, that in his Jewish pride he overrated and even misunderstood Christianity. He all but overlooked the narrow connection between Christianity and Democracy. He did not see that in fighting Liberalism and Nonconformity all his life, he was really fighting Christianity, the Protestant Form of which is at the root of British Liberalism and Individualism to this very day. And when later in his life Disraeli complained that the disturbance in the mind of nations has been occasioned by "the powerful assault on the Divinity of the Semitic Literature by the Germans," he overlooked likewise the connection of this German movement with the same Protestantism, from the narrow and vulgar middle-class of which have sprung all those rationalising, unimaginative, and merely clever professors, who have so successfully undermined the ancient and venerable lore. And thirdly, and worst of all, Disraeli never suspected that the French Revolution, which in the same breath he once contemptuously denounced as "the Celtic Rebellion against Semitic laws," was, in spite of its professed attack against religion, really a profoundly Christian, because a democratic and revolutionary movement. What a pity he did not know all this! What a shower of splendid additional sarcasms he would have poured over those flat-nosed Franks, had he known what I know now, that it is the eternal way of the Christian to be a rebel, and that just as he has once rebelled against us, he has never ceased pestering and rebelling against any one else either of his own or any other creed.

But it is so easy for me to be carried away by that favourite sport of mine, of which I am the first inventor among the Jews—Christian baiting. You must forgive this, however, in a Jew, who, while he has been baited for two thousand years by you, likes to turn round now that the opportunity has come, and tries to indulge on his part also in a little bit of that genial pastime. I candidly confess it is delightful, and I now quite understand your ancestors hunting mine as much as they could—had I been a Christian, I would, probably, have done the same; perhaps have done it even better, for no one would now be left to write any such impudent truisms against me— rest assured of that! But as I am a Jew, and have had too much experience of the other side of the question, I must try to control myself in the midst of victory; I must judge things calmly; I must state fact honestly; I must not allow myself to be unjust towards you. First of all, then, this rebelling faculty of yours is a Jewish inheritance, an inheritance, however, of which you have made a more than generous, a truly Christian use, because you did not keep it niggardly for yourselves, but have distributed it all over the earth, from Nazareth to Nishni-Novgorod, from Jerusalem to Jamaica, from Palestine to Pimlico, so that every one is a rebel and an anarchist nowadays. But, secondly, I must not forget that in every Anarchist, and therefore in every Christian, there is also, or may be, an aristocrat—a man who, just like the anarchist, but with a perfectly holy right, wishes to obey no laws but those of his own conscience; a man who thinks too highly of his own faith and persuasion, to convert other people to it; a man who, therefore, would never carry it to Caffres and Coolis; a man, in short, with whom even the noblest and exclusive Hebrew could shake hands. In Friedrich Nietzsche this aristocratic element which may be hidden in a Christian has been brought to light, in him the Christian's eternal claim for freedom of conscience, for his own priesthood, for justification by his own faith, is no longer used for purposes of destruction and rebellion, but for those of command and creation; in him—and this is the key to the character of this extraordinary man, who both on his father's and mother's side was the descendant of a long line of Protestant Parsons— the Christian and Protestant spirit of anarchy became so strong that he rebelled even against his own fellow-Anarchists, and told them that Anarchy was a low and contemptible thing, and that Revolution was an occupation fit only for superior slaves. But with this event the circle of Christianity has become closed, and the exclusive House of Israel is now under the delightful obligation to make its peace with its once lost and now reforming son.

The venerable Owner of this old house is still standing on its threshold: his face is pale, his expression careworn, his eyes apparently scanning something far in the distance. The wind—for there is a terrible wind blowing just now— is playing havoc with his long white Jew-beard, but this white Jew-beard of his is growing black again at the end, and even the sad eyes are still capable of quite youthful flashes, as may be noticed at this very moment. For the eyes of the old Jew, apparently so dreamy and so far away, have suddenly become fixed upon something in the distance yonder. The old Jew looks and looks— and then he rubs his eyes—and then he eagerly looks again. And now he is sure of himself. His old and haggard face is lighting up, his stooped figure suddenly becomes more erect, and a tear of joy is seen running over his pale cheek into that long beard of his. For the old Jew has recognised some one coming from afar—some one whom he had missed, but never mentioned, for his Law forbade him to do this—some one, however, for whom he had secretly always mourned, as only the race of the psalmists and the prophets can mourn—and he rushes toward him, and he falls on his neck and he kisses him, and he says to his servants: "Bring forth the best robe and put it on him, and put a ring on his hand and shoes on his feet. And bring hither the fatted calf, and kill it and let us eat and be merry!" AMEN.

OSCAR LEVY.

LONDON, *January* 1909.

TRANSLATOR'S PREFACE.

To the reader who knows Nietzsche, who has studied his *Zarathustra* and understood it, and who, in addition, has digested the works entitled *Beyond Good and Evil*, *The Genealogy of Morals*, *The Twilight of the Idols*, and *The Antichrist*,— to such a reader everything in this volume will be perfectly clear and comprehensible. In the attack on Strauss he will immediately detect the germ of the whole of Nietzsche's subsequent attitude towards too hasty contentment and the foolish beatitude of the "easily pleased"; in the paper on Wagner he will recognise Nietzsche the indefatigable borer, miner and underminer, seeking to define his ideals, striving after self-knowledge above all, and availing himself of any contemporary approximation to his ideal man, in order to press it forward as the incarnation of his thoughts. Wagner the reformer of mankind! Wagner the dithyrambic dramatist!—The reader who knows Nietzsche will not be misled by these expressions.

To the uninitiated reader, however, some words of explanation are due, not only in regard to the two papers before us, but in regard to Nietzsche himself. So much in our time is learnt from hearsay concerning prominent figures in science, art, religion, or philosophy, that it is hardly possible for anybody to-day, however badly informed he may be, to begin the study of any great writer or scientist with a perfectly open mind. It were well, therefore, to begin the study of Nietzsche with some definite idea as to his unaltered purpose, if he ever possessed such a thing; as to his lifelong ideal, if he ever kept one so long; and as to the one direction in which he always travelled, despite apparent deviations and windings. Had he such a purpose, such an ideal, such a direction? We have no wish to open a controversy here, neither do we think that in replying to this question in the affirmative we shall give rise to one; for every careful student of Nietzsche, we know, will uphold us in our view. Nietzsche had one very definite and unaltered purpose, ideal and direction, and this was "the elevation of the type man." He tells us in *The Will to Power*: "All is truth to me that tends to elevate man!" To this principle he was already pledged as a student at Leipzig; we owe every line that he ever wrote to his devotion to it, and it is the key to all his complexities, blasphemies, prolixities, and terrible earnestness. All was good to Nietzsche that tended to elevate man; all was bad that kept man stationary or sent him backwards. Hence he wrote *David Strauss, the Confessor and Writer* (1873).

The Franco-German War had only just come to an end, and the keynote of this polemical pamphlet is, "Beware of the intoxication of success." When the whole of Germany was delirious with joy over her victory, at a time when the unquestioned triumph of her arms tended rather to reflect unearned glory upon every department of her social organisation, it required both courage and discernment to raise the warning voice and to apply the wet blanket. But Nietzsche did both, and with spirit, because his worst fears were aroused. Smug content (*erbärmliches Behagen*) was threatening to thwart his one purpose—the elevation of man; smug content personified in the German scholar was giving itself airs of omniscience, omnipotence, and ubiquity, and all the while it was a mere cover for hidden rottenness and jejune pedantry.

Nietzsche's attack on Hegelian optimism alone (pp. 46, 53-54), in the first paper, fully reveals the fundamental idea underlying this essay; and if the personal attack on Strauss seems sometimes to throw the main theme into the background, we must remember the author's own attitude towards this aspect of the case. Nietzsche, as a matter of fact, had neither the spite nor the meanness requisite for the purely personal attack. In his *Ecce Homo*, he tells us most emphatically: "I have no desire to attack particular persons—I do but use a personality as a magnifying glass; I place it over the subject to which I wish to call attention, merely that the appeal may be stronger." David Strauss, in a letter to a friend, soon after the publication of the first *Thought out of Season*, expresses his utter astonishment that a total stranger should have made such a dead set at him. The same problem may possibly face the reader on every page of this fssay: if, however, we realise Nietzsche's purpose, if we understand his struggle to be one against "Culture-Philistinism" in general, as a stemming, stultifying and therefore degenerate factor, and regard David Strauss—as the author himself did, that is to say, simply as a glass, focusing the whole light of our understanding upon the main theme— then the Strauss paper is seen to be one of such enormous power, and its aim appears to us so lofty, that, whatever our views may be concerning the nature of the person assailed, we are forced to conclude that, to Nietzsche at least, he was but the incarnation and concrete example of the evil and danger then threatening to overtake his country, which it was the object of this essay to expose.

When we read that at the time of Strauss's death (February 7th, 1874) Nietzsche was greatly tormented by the fear that the old scholar might have been hastened to his end by the use that had been made of his personality in the first *Unzeitgemässe Betrachtung*; when we remember that in the midst of this torment he ejaculated, "I was indeed not made to hate and have enemies!"— we are then in a better position to judge of the motives which, throughout his life, led him to engage such formidable opponents and to undertake such relentless attacks. It was merely his ruling principle that, all is true and good that tends to elevate man; everything is bad and false that keeps man stationary or sends him backwards.

Those who may think that his attacks were often unwarrantable and ill-judged will do well, therefore, to bear this in mind, that whatever his value or merits may have been as an iconoclast, at least the aim he had was sufficiently lofty and honourable, and that he never shirked the duties which he rightly or wrongly imagined would help him to

Wagner paper (1875-1876) we are faced by a somewhat different problem. Most readers who will have heard of Nietzsche's subsequent denunciation of Wagner's music will probably stand aghast before this panegyric of him; those who, like Professor Saintsbury, will fail to discover the internal evidence in this essay which points so infallibly to Nietzsche's *real* but still subconscious opinion of his hero, may even be content to regard his later attitude as the result of a complete *volte-face*, and at any rate a flat contradiction of the one revealed in this paper. Let us, however, examine the internal evidence we speak of, and let us also discuss the purpose and spirit of the essay.

We have said that Nietzsche was a man with a very fixed and powerful ideal, and we have heard what this ideal was. Can we picture him, then,—a young and enthusiastic scholar with a cultured love of music, and particularly of Wagner's music, eagerly scanning all his circle, the whole city and country in which he lived—yea, even the whole continent on which he lived—for something or some one that would set his doubts at rest concerning the feasibility of his ideal? Can we now picture this young man coming face to face with probably one of the greatest geniuses of his age—with a man whose very presence must have been electric, whose every word or movement must have imparted some power to his surroundings—with Richard Wagner?

If we can conceive of what the mere attention, even, of a man like Wagner must have meant to Nietzsche in his twenties, if we can form any idea of the intoxicating effect produced upon him when this attention developed into friendship, we almost refuse to believe that Nietzsche could have been critical at all at first. In Wagner, as was but natural, he soon began to see the ideal, or at least the means to the ideal, which was his one obsession. All his hope for the future of Germany and Europe cleaved, as it were, to this highest manifestation of their people's life, and gradually he began to invest his already great friend with all the extra greatness which he himself drew from the depths of his own soul.

The friendship which grew between them was of that rare order in which neither can tell who influences the other more. Wagner would often declare that the beautiful music in the third act of Siegfried was to be ascribed to Nietzsche's influence over him; he also adopted the young man's terminology in art matters, and the concepts implied by the words "Dionysian" and "Apollonian" were borrowed by him from his friend's discourses. How much Nietzsche owed to Wagner may perhaps never be definitely known; to those who are sufficiently interested to undertake the investigation of this matter, we would recommend Hans Belart's book, *Nietzsche's Ethik*; in it references will be found which give some clue as to the probable sources from which the necessary information may be derived. In any case, however, the reciprocal effects of their conversations will never be exactly known; and although it would be ridiculous to assume that Nietzsche was essentially the same when he left as when he met him, what the real nature of the change was it is now difficult to say.

For some years their friendship continued firm, and grew ever more and more intimate. *The Birth Of Tragedy* was one of the first public declarations of it, and after its publication many were led to consider that Wagner's art was a sort of resurrection of the Dionysian Grecian art. Enemies of Nietzsche began to whisper that he was merely Wagner's "literary lackey"; many friends frowned upon the promising young philologist, and questioned the exaggerated importance he was beginning to ascribe to the art of music and to art in general, in their influence upon the world; and all the while Nietzsche's one thought and one aim was to help the cause and further the prospects of the man who he earnestly believed was destined to be the salvation of European culture.

Every great ideal coined in his own brain he imagined to be the ideal of his hero; all his sublimest hopes for society were presented gratis, in his writings, to Wagner, as though products of the latter's own mind; and just as the prophet of old never possessed the requisite assurance to suppose that his noblest ideas were his own, but attributed them to some higher and supernatural power, whom he thereby learnt to worship for its fancied nobility of sentiment, so Nietzsche, still doubting his own powers, created a fetich out of nis most distinguished friend, and was ultimately wounded and well-nigh wrecked with disappointment when he found that the Wagner of the Gotterdammerung and Parsifal was not the Wagner of his own mind.

While writing *Ecce Homo*, he was so well aware of the extent to which he had gone in idealising his friend, that he even felt able to say: "*Wagner in Bayreuth* is a vision of my own future.... Now that I can look back upon this work, I would not like to deny that, at bottom, it speaks only of myself" (p. 74). And on another page of the same book we read: "... What I heard, as a young man, in Wagnerian music, had absolutely nothing to do with Wagner: when I described Dionysian music, I only described what *I* had heard, and I thus translated and transfigured all that I bore in my own soul into the spirit of the new art. The strongest proof of this is my essay, *Wagner in Bayreuth*: in all decidedly psychological passages of this book the reader may simply read my name, or the name 'Zarathustra,' wherever the text contains the name 'Wagner'" (p. 68).

As we have already hinted, there are evidences of his having subconsciously discerned the REAL Wagner, even in the heyday of their friendship, behind the ideal he had formed of him; for his eyes were too intelligent to be deceived, even though his understanding refused at first to heed the messages they sent it: both the *Birth of Tragedy* and *Wagner in Bayreuth* are with us to prove this, and not merely when we read these works between the lines, but when we take such passages as those found on pp. 115, 149, 150, 151, 156, 158, 159 of this book quite literally.

Nietzsche's infatuation we have explained; the consequent idealisation of the object of his infatuation he himself has confessed; we have also pointed certain passages which we believe show beyond a doubt that almost everything to be found in *The Case of Wagner* and *Nietzsche contra Wagner* was already subconscious in our author, long before he had begun to feel even a coolness towards his hero: let those who think our interpretation of the said passages is either strained or unjustified turn to the literature to which we have referred and judge for themselves. It seems to us that those distinguished critics who complain of Nietzsche's complete *volte-face* and his uncontrollable recantations and revulsions of feeling have completely overlooked this aspect of the question.

It were well for us to bear in mind that we are not altogether free to dispose of Nietzsche's attitude to Wagner, at any given period in their relationship, with a single sentence of praise or of blame. After all, we are faced by a problem which no objectivity or dispassionate detachment on our parts can solve. Nietzsche endowed both Schopenhauer and Wagner with qualities and aspirations so utterly foreign to them both, that neither of them would have recognised himself in the images he painted of them. His love for them was unusual; perhaps it can only be fully understood emotionally by us: like all men who are capable of very great love, Nietzsche lent the objects of his affection anything they might happen to lack in the way of greatness, and when at last his eyes were opened, genuine pain, not malice, was the motive of even the most bitter of his diatribes.

Finally, we should just like to give one more passage from *Ecce Homo* bearing upon the subject under discussion. It is particularly interesting from an autobiographical standpoint, and will perhaps afford the best possible conclusion to this preface.

Nietzsche is writing about Wagner's music, and he says: "The world must indeed be empty for him who has never been unhealthy enough for this 'infernal voluptuousness'; it is allowable and yet almost forbidden to use a mystical expression in this behalf. I suppose I know better than any one the prodigies Wagner was capable of, the fifty worlds of strange raptures to which no one save him could soar; and as I stand to-day—strong enough to convert even the most suspicious and dangerous phenomenon to my own use and be the stronger for it—I declare Wagner to be the great benefactor of my life. Something will always keep our names associated in the minds of men, and that is, that we are two who have suffered more excruciatingly— even at each other's hands—than most men are able to suffer nowadays. And just as Wagner is merely a misunderstanding among Germans, so am I and ever will be. You lack two centuries of psychological and artistic discipline, my dear countrymen!... But it will be impossible for you ever to recover the time now lost" (p. 43).

ANTHONY M. LUDOVICI.

DAVID STRAUSS,

THE CONFESSOR AND THE WRITER.

DAVID STRAUSS

I.

Public opinion in Germany seems strictly to forbid any allusion to the evil and dangeious consequences of a war, more particularly when the war in question has been a victorious one. Those writers, therefore, command a more ready attention who, regarding this public opinion as final, proceed to vie with each other in their jubilant praise of the war, and of the powerful influences it has brought to bear upon morality, culture, and art. Yet it must be confessed that a gieat victory is a great danger. Human nature bears a triumph less easily than a defeat; indeed, it might even be urged that it is simpler to gain a victory of this sort than to turn it to such account that it may not ultimately proxe a seiious rout.

But of all evil results due to the last contest with France, the most deplorable, peihaps, is that widespread and even universal error of public opinion and of all who think publicly, that German culture was also victorious in the struggle, and that it should now, therefore, be decked with garlands, as a fit recognition of such extraordinary events and successes. This error is in the highest degree pernicious: not because it is an error,—for there are illusions which are both salutary and blessed,—but because it threatens to convert our victory into a signal defeat. A defeat? —I should say rather, into the uprooting of the "German Mind" for the benefit of the "German Empire."

Even supposing that the fight had been between the two cultures, the standard for the value of the victor would still be a very relative one, and, in any case, would certainly not justify such exaggerated triumph or self-glorification. For, in the first place, it would be necessary to ascertain the worth of the conquered culture. This might be very little; in which case, even if the victory had involved the most glorious display of arms, it would still offer no warrant for inordinate rapture.

Even so, however, there can be no question, in our case, of the victory of German culture; and for the simple reason, that French culture remains as heretofore, and that we depend upon it as heretofore. It did not even help towards the success of our arms. Severe military discipline, natural bravery and sustaining power, the superior generalship, unity and obedience in the rank and file—in short, factors which have nothing to do with culture, were instrumental in making us conquer an opponent in whom the most essential of these factors were absent. The only wonder is, that precisely what is now called "culture" in Germany did not prove an obstacle to the military operations which seemed vitally necessary to a great victory. Perhaps, though, this was only owing to the fact that this "thing" which dubs itself "culture" saw its advantage, for once, in keeping in the background.

If however, it be permitted to grow and to spread, if it be spoilt by the flattering and nonsensical assurance that *it* has been victorious,—then, as I have said, it will have the power to extirpate German mind, and, when that is done, who knows whether there will still be anything to be made out of the surviving German body!

Provided it were possible to direct that calm and tenacious bravery which the German opposed to the pathetic and spontaneous fury of the Frenchman, against the inward enemy, against the highly suspicious and, at all events, unnative "cultivation" which, owing to a dangerous misunderstanding, is called "culture" in Germany, then all hope of a really genuine German "culture"—the reverse of that "cultivation"—would not be entirely lost. For the Germans have never known any lack of clear-sighted and heroic leaders, though these, often enough, probably, have lacked Germans. But whether it be possible to turn German bravery into a new direction seems to me to become ever more and more doubtful; for I realise how fully convinced every one is that such a struggle and such bravery are no longer requisite; on the contrary, that most things are regulated as satisfactorily as they possibly can be—or, at all events, that everything of moment has long ago been discovered and accomplished: in a word, that the seed of culture is already sown everywhere, and is now either shooting up its fresh green blades, or, here and there, even bursting forth into luxuriant blossom. In this sphere, not only happiness but ecstasy reigns supreme. I am conscious of this ecstasy and happiness, in the ineffable, truculent assurance of German journalists and manufacturers of novels, tragedies, poems, and histories (for it must be clear that these people belong to one category), who seem to have conspired to improve the leisure and ruminative hours—that is to say, "the intellectual lapses"—of the modern man, by bewildering him with their printed paper. Since the war, all is gladness, dignity, and self-consciousness in this merry throng. After the startling successes of German culture, it regards itself, not only as approved and sanctioned, but almost as sanctified. It therefore speaks with gravity, affects to apostrophise the German People, and issues complete works, after the manner of the classics; nor does it shrink from proclaiming in those journals which are open to it some few of its adherents as new German classical writers and model authors. It might be supposed that the dangers of such an *abuse of success* would be recognised by the more thoughtful and enlightened among cultivated Germans; or, at least, that these would feel how painful is the comedy that is being enacted around them: for what in truth could more readily inspire pity than the sight of a cripple strutting like a cock before a mirror, and exchanging complacent glances with his reflection! But the "scholar" caste willingly allow things to remain as they are, and re too much concerned with their own affairs to busy themselves with the care of the German mind. Moreover, the units of this caste are too thoroughly convinced that their own scholarship is the ripest and most perfect fruit of the age—in fact, of all ages—to see any necessity for a care of German culture in general; since, in so far as they and the legion of their brethren are concerned, preoccupations of this order have everywhere been, so to speak, surpassed. The more conscientious observer, more particularly if he be a foreigner, cannot help noticing withal that no great disparity exists between that which the German scholar regards as his culture and that other triumphant culture of the new German classics, save in respect of the quantum of knowledge. Everywhere, where knowledge and not ability, where information and not art, hold the first rank,—everywhere, therefore, where life bears testimony to the kind of culture extant, there is now only one specific German culture—and this is the culture that is supposed to have conquered France?

The contention appears to be altogether too preposterous. It was solely to the more extensive knowledge of German officers, to the superior training of their soldiers, and to their more scientific military strategy, that all impartial Judges, and even the French nation, in the end, ascribed the victory. Hence, if it be intended to regard German erudition as a thing apart, in what sense can German culture be said to have conquered? In none whatsoever; for the moral qualities of severe discipline, of more placid obedience, have nothing in common with culture: these were characteristic of the Macedonian army, for instance, despite the fact that the Greek soldiers were infinitely more cultivated. To speak of German scholarship and culture as having conquered, therefore, can only be the outcome of a misapprehension, probably resulting from the circumstance that every precise notion of culture has now vanished from Germany.

Culture is, before all things, the unity of artistic style, in every expression of the life of a people. Abundant knowledge and learning, however, are not essential to it, nor are they a sign of its existence; and, at a pinch, they might coexist much more harmoniously with the very opposite of culture—with barbarity: that is to say, with a complete lack of style, or with a riotous jumble of all styles. But it is precisely amid this riotous jumble that the German of to-day subsists; and the serious problem to be solved is: how, with all his learning, he can possibly avoid noticing it; how, into the bargain, he can rejoice with all his heart in his present "culture"? For everything conduces to open his eyes for him—every glance he casts at his clothes, his room, his house; every walk he takes through the streets of his town; every visit he pays to his art-dealers and to his trader in the articles of fashion. In his social intercourse he ought to realise the origin of his manners and movements; in the heart of our art-institutions, the pleasures of our concerts, theatres, and museums, he ought to become apprised of the super- and juxta-position of all imaginable styles. The German heaps up around him the forms, colours, products, and curiosities of all ages and zones, and thereby succeeds in producing that garish newness, as of a country fair, which his scholars then proceed to contemplate and to define as "Modernism *per se*"; and there he remains, squatting peacefully, in the midst of this conflict of styles. But with this kind of culture, which is, at bottom, nothing more nor less than a phlegmatic insensibility to real culture, men cannot vanquish an enemy, least of all an enemy like the French, who, whatever their worth may be, do actually possess a genuine and productive culture, and whom, up to the present, we have systematically copied, though in the majority of cases without skill.

Even supposing we had really ceased copying them, it would still not mean that we had overcome them, but merely that we had lifted their yoke from our necks. Not before we have succeeded in forcing an original German culture upon them can there be any question of the triumph of German culture. Meanwhile, let us not forget that in all matters of form we are, and must be, just as dependent upon Paris now as we were before the war; for up to the present there has been no such thing as a original German culture.

We all ought to have become aware of this, of our own accord. Besides, one of the few who had he right to speak to Germans in terms of reproach Publicly drew attention to the fact. "We Germans are of yesterday," Goethe once said to Eckermann. "True, for the last hundred years we have diligently cultivated ourselves, but a few centuries may yet have to run their course before our fellow-countrymen become permeated with sufficient intellectuality and higher culture to have it said of them, *it is a long time since they were barbarians.*"

II.

If, however, our public and private life is so manifestly devoid of all signs of a productive and characteristic culture; if, moreover, our great artists, with that earnest vehemence and honesty which is peculiar to greatness admit, and have admitted, this monstrous fact—so very humiliating to a gifted nation; how can it still be possible for contentment to reign to such an astonishing extent among German scholars? And since the last war this complacent spirit has seemed ever more and morerready to break forth into exultant cries and demonstrations of triumph. At all events, the belief seems to be rife that we are in possession of a genuine culture, and the enormous incongruity of this triumphant satisfaction in the face of the inferiority which should be patent to all, seems only to be noticed by the few and the select. For all those who think with the public mind have blindfolded their eyes and closed their ears. The incongruity is not even acknowledged to exist. How is this possible? What power is sufficiently influential to deny this existence? What species of men must have attained to supremacy in Germany that feelings which are so strong and simple should he denied or prevented from obtaining expression? This power, this species of men, I will name—they are the *Philistines of Culture.*

As every one knows, the word "Philistine" is borrowed from the vernacular of student-life, and, in its widest and most popular sense, it signifies the reverse of a son of the Muses, of an artist, and of the genuine man of culture. The Philistine of culture, however, the study of whose type and the hearing of whose confessions (when he makes them) have now become tiresome duties, distinguishes himself from the general notion of the order "Philistine" by means of a superstition: he fancies that he is himself a son of the Muses and a man of culture. This incomprehensible error clearly shows that he does not even know the difference between a Philistine and his opposite. We must not be surprised, therefore, if we find him, for the most part, solemnly protesting that he is no Philistine. Owing to this lack of self-knowledge, he is convinced that his "culture" is the consummate manifestation of real German culture; and, since he everywhere meets with scholars of his own type, since all public institutions, whether schools, universities, or academies, are so organised as to be in complete harmony with his education and needs, wherever he goes he bears with him the triumphant feeling that he is the worthy champion of prevailing German culture, and he frames his pretensions and claims accordingly.

If, however, real culture takes unity of style for granted (and even an inferior and degenerate culture cannot be imagined in which a certain coalescence of the profusion of forms has not taken place), it is just possible that the confusion underlying the Culture-Philistine's error may arise from the fact that, since he comes into contact everywhere with creatures cast in the same mould as himself, he concludes that this uniformity among all "scholars" must point to a certain uniformity in German education—hence to culture. All round him, he sees only needs and views similar to his own; wherever he goes, he finds himself embraced by a ring of tacit conventions concerning almost everything, but more especially matters of religion and art. This imposing sameness, this *tutti unisono* which, though it responds to no word of command, is yet ever ready to burst forth, cozens him into the belief that here a culture must be established and flourishing. But Philistinism, despite its systematic organisation and power, does not constitute a culture by virtue of its system alone; it does not even constitute an inferior culture, but invariably the reverse—namely, firmly established barbarity. For the uniformity of character which is so apparent in the German scholars of to-day is only the result of a conscious or unconscious exclusion and negation of all the artistically productive forms and requirements of a genuine style. The mind of the cultured Philistine must have become sadly unhinged; for precisely what culture repudiates he regards as culture itself; and, since he proceeds logically, he succeeds in creating a connected group of these repudiations—a system of non-culture, to which one might at a pinch grant a certain "unity of style," provided of course it were Ot nonsense to attribute style to barbarity. If he have to choose between a stylish act and its opposite, he will invariably adopt the latter, and, since this rule holds good throughout, every one of his acts bears the same negative stamp. Now, it is by means of this stamp that he is able to identify the character of the "German culture," which is his own patent; and all things that do not bear it are so many enemies and obstacles drawn up against him. In the presence of these arrayed forces the Culture-Philistine either does no more than ward off the blows, or else he denies, holds his tongue, stops his ears, and refuses to face facts. He is a negative creature—even in his hatred and animosity. Nobody, however, is more disliked by him than the man who regards him as a Philistine, and tells him what he is—namely, the barrier in the way of all powerful men and creators, the labyrinth for all who doubt and go astray, the swamp for all the weak and the weary, the fetters of those who would run towards lofty goals, the poisonous mist that chokes all germinating hopes, the scorching sand to all those German thinkers who seek for, and thirst after, a new life. For the mind of Germany is seeking; and ye hate it because it is seeking, and because it will not accept your word, when ye declare that ye have found what it is seeking. How could it have been possible for a type like that of the Culture-Philistine to develop? and even granting its development, how was it able to rise to the powerful Position of supreme judge concerning all questions of German culture? How could this have been possible, seeing that a whole procession of grand and heroic figures has already filed past us, whose every movement, the expression of whose every feature, whose questioning voice and burning eye betrayed the one fact, *that they were seekers*, and that they sought that which the Culture-Philistine had long fancied he had found—to wit, a genuine original German culture? Is there a soil—thus they seemed to ask—a soil that is pure enough, unhandselled enough, of sufficient virgin sanctity, to allow the mind of Germany to build its house upon it? Questioning thus, they wandered through the wilderness, and the woods of wretched ages and narrow conditions, and as seekers they disappeared from our vision; one of them, at an advanced age, was even able to say, in the name of all: "For half a century my life has been hard and bitter enough; I have allowed myself no rest, but have ever striven, sought and done, to the best and to the utmost of my ability."

What does our Culture-Philistinism say of these seekers? It regards them simply as discoverers, and seems to forget that they themselves only claimed to be seekers. We have our culture, say her sons; for have we not our "classics"? Not only is the foundation there, but the building already stands upon it—we ourselves constitute that building. And, so saying, the Philistine raises his hand to his brow.

But, in order to be able thus to misjudge, and thus to grant left-handed veneration to our classics, people must have ceased to know them. This, generally speaking, is precisely what has happened. For, otherwise, one ought to know that there is only one way of honouring them, and that is to continue seeking with the same spirit and with the same courage, and not to weary of the search. But to foist the doubtful title of "classics" upon them, and to "edify" oneself from time to time by reading their works, means to yield to those feeble and selfish emotions which all the paying public may purchase at concert-halls and theatres. Even the raising of monuments to their memory, and the christening of feasts and societies with their names—all these things are but so many ringing cash payments by means of which the Culture-Philistine discharges his indebtedness to them, so that in all other respects he may be rid of them, and, above all, not bound to follow in their wake and prosecute his search further. For henceforth inquiry is to cease: that is the Philistine watchword.

This watchword once had some meaning. In Germany, during the first decade of the nineteenth century, for instance, when the heyday and confusion of seeking, experimenting, destroying, promising, surmising, and hoping was sweeping in currents and cross-currents over the land, the thinking middle-classes were right in their concern for their own security. It was then quite right of them to dismiss from their minds with a shrug of their shoulders the *omnium gatherum* of fantastic and language-maiming philosophies, and of rabid special-pleading historical studies, the carnival of all gods and myths, and the poetical affectations and fooleries which a drunken spirit may be responsible for. In this respect they were quite right; for the Philistine has not even the privilege of licence. With the cunning proper to base natures, however, he availed himself of the opportunity, in order to throw suspicion even upon the seeking spirit, and to invite people to join in the more comfortable pastime of finding. His eye opened to the joy of Philistinism; he saved himself from wild experimenting by clinging to the idyllic, and opposed the restless creative spirit that animates the artist, by means of a certain smug ease—the ease of self-conscious narrowness, tranquillity, and self-sufficiency. His tapering finger pointed, without any affectation of modesty, to all the hidden and intimate incidents of his life, to the many touching and ingenuous joys which sprang into existence in the wretched depths of his uncultivated existence, and which modestly blossomed forth on the bog-land of Philistinism.

There were, naturally, a few gifted narrators who, with a nice touch, drew vivid pictures of the happiness, the prosaic simplicity, the bucolic robustness, and all the well-being which floods the quarters of children, scholars, and peasants. With picture-books of this class in their hands, these smug ones now once and for all sought to escape from the yoke of these dubious classics and the command which they contained—to seek further and to find. They only started the notion of an epigone-age in order to secure peace for themselves, and to be able to reject all the efforts of disturbing innovators summarily as the work of epigones. With the view of ensuring their own tranquillity, these smug ones even appropriated history, and sought to transform all sciences that threatened to disturb their wretched ease into branches of history—more particularly philosophy and classical philology. Through historical consciousness, they saved themselves from enthusiasm; for, in opposition to Goethe, it was maintained that history would no longer kindle enthusiasm. No, in their desire to acquire an historical grasp of everything, stultification became the sole aim of these philosophical admirers of "*nil admirari*." While professing to hate every form of fanaticism and intolerance, what they really hated, at bottom, was the dominating genius and the tyranny of the real claims of culture. They therefore concentrated and utilised all their forces in those quarters where a fresh and vigorous movement was to be expected, and then paralysed, stupefied, and tore it to shreds. In this way, a philosophy which veiled the Philistine confessions of its founder beneath neat twists and flourishes of language proceeded further to discover a formula for the canonisation of the commonplace. It expatiated upon the rationalism of all reality, and thus ingratiated itself with the Culture-Philistine, who also loves neat twists and flourishes, and who, above all, considers himself real, and regards his reality as the standard of reason for the world. From this time forward he began to allow every one, and even himself, to reflect, to investigate, to astheticise, and, more particularly, to make poetry, music, and even pictures—not to mention systems philosophy; provided, of course, that everything were done according to the old pattern, and that no assault were made upon the "reasonable" and the "real"—that is to say, upon the Philistine. The latter really does not at all mind giving himself up, from time to time, to the delightful and daring transgressions of art or of sceptical historical studies, and he does not underestimate the charm of such recreations and entertainments; but he strictly separates "the earnestness of life" (under which term he understands his calling, his business, and his wife and child) from such trivialities, and among the latter he includes all things which have any relation to culture. Therefore, woe to the art that takes itself seriously, that has a notion of what it may exact, and that dares to endanger his income, his business, and his habits! Upon such an art he turns his back, as though it were something dissolute; and, affecting the attitude of a. guardian of chastity, he cautions every unprotected virtue on no account to look.

Being such an adept at cautioning people, he is always grateful to any artist who heeds him and listens to caution. He then assures his protege that things are to be made more easy for him; that, as a kindred spirit, he will no longer be expected to make sublime masterpieces, but that his work must be one of two kinds—either the imitation of reality to the point of simian mimicry, in idylls or gentle and humorous satires, or the free copying of the best-known and most famous classical works, albeit with shamefast concessions to the taste of the age. For, although he may only be able to appreciate slavish copying or accurate portraiture of the present, still he knows that the latter will but glorify him, and increase the well-being of "reality"; while the former, far from doing him any harm, rather helps to establish his reputation as a classical judge of taste, and is not otherwise troublesome; for he has, once and for all, come to terms with the classics. Finally, he discovers the general and effective formula "Health" for his habits, methods of observation, judgments, and the objects of his patronage; while he dismisses the importunate disturber of the peace with the epithets "hysterical" and "morbid." It is thus that David Strauss—a genuine example of the *satisfait* in regard to our scholastic institutions, and a typical Philistine—it is thus that he speaks of "the philosophy of Schopenhauer" as being "thoroughly intellectual, yet often unhealthy and unprofitable." It is indeed a deplorable fact that intellect should show such a decided preference for the "unhealthy" and the "unprofitable"; and even the Philistine, if he be true to himself, will admit that, in regard to the philosophies which men of his stamp produce, he is conscious of a frequent lack of intellectuality, although of course they are always thoroughly healthy and profitable.

Now and again, the Philistines, provided they are by themselves, indulge in a bottle of wine, and then they grow reminiscent, and speak of the great deeds of the war, honestly and ingenuously. On such occasions it often happens that a great deal comes to light which would otherwise have been most stead-fastly concealed, and one of them may even be heard to blurt out the most precious secrets of the whole brotherhood. Indeed, a lapse of this sort occurred but a short while ago, to a well-known aesthete of the Hegelian school of reasoning. It must, however, be admitted that the provocation thereto was of an unusual character. A company of Philistines were feasting together, in celebration of the memory of a genuine anti-Philistine—one who, moreover, had been, in the strictest sense of the words, wrecked by Philistinism. This man was Holderlin, and the afore-mentioned aesthete was therefore justified, under the circumstances, in speaking of the tragic souls who had foundered on "reality"—reality being understood, here, to mean

Philistine reason. But the "reality" is now different, and it might well be asked whether Holderlin would be able to find his way at all in the present great age. "I doubt," says Dr. Vischer, "whether his delicate soul could have borne all the roughness which is inseparable from war, and whether it had survived the amount of perversity which, since the war, we now see flourishing in every quarter. Perhaps he would have succumbed to despair. His was one of the unarmed souls; he was the Werther of Greece, a hopeless lover; his life was full of softness and yearning, but there was strength and substance in his will, and in his style, greatness, riches and life; here and there it is even reminiscent of AEschylus. His spirit, however, lacked hardness. He lacked the weapon humour; he could not grant that one may be a Philistine and still be no barbarian." Not the sugary condolence of the post-prandial speaker, but this last sentence concerns us. Yes, it is admitted that one is a Philistine; but, a barbarian?—No, not at any price! Unfortunately, poor Holderlin could not make such flne distinctions. If one reads the reverse of civilisation, or perhaps sea-pirating, or cannibalism, into the word "barbarian," then the distinction is justifiable enough. But what the aesthete obviously wishes to prove to us is, that we may be Philistines and at the same time men of culture. Therein lies the humour which poor Holderlin lacked and the need of which ultimately wrecked him.*

[Footnote * : Nietzsche's allusion to Holderlin here is full of tragic significance; for, like Holderlin, he too was ultimately wrecked and driven insane by the Philistinism of his age. —Translator's note.]

On this occasion a second admission was made by the speaker: "It is not always strength of will, but weakness, which makes us superior to those tragic souls which are so passionately responsive to the attractions of beauty," or words to this effect. And this was said in the name of the assembled "We"; that is to say, the "superiors," the "superiors through weakness." Let us content ourselves with these admissions. We are now in possession of information concerning two matters from one of the initiated: first, that these "We" stand beyond the passion for beauty; secondly, that their position was reached by means of weakness. In less confidential moments, however, it was just this weakness which masqueraded in the guise of a much more beautiful name: it was the famous "healthiness" of the Culture-Philistine. In view of this very recent restatement of the case, however, it would be as well not to speak of them any longer as the "healthy ones," but as the "weakly," or, still better, as the "feeble." Oh, if only these feeble ones were not in power! How is it that they concern themselves at all about what we call them! They are the rulers, and he is a poor ruler who cannot endure to be called by a nickname. Yes, if one only have power, one soon learns to poke fun—even at oneself. It cannot matter so very much, therefore, even if one do give oneself away; for what could not the purple mantle of triumph conceal? The strength of the Culture-Philistine steps into the broad light of day when he acknowledges his weakness; and the more he acknowledges it— the more cynically he acknowledges it—the more completely he betrays his consciousness of his own importance and superiority. We are living in a period of cynical Philistine confessions. Just as Friedrich Vischer gave us his in a word, so has David Strauss handed us his in a book; and both that word and that book are cynical.

III.

Concerning Culture-Philistinism, David Strauss makes a double confession, by word and by deed; that is to say, by the word of the confessor, and the act of the writer. His book entitled *The Old Faith and the New* is, first in regard to its contents, and secondly in regard to its being a book and a literary production, an uninterrupted confession; while, in the very fact that he allows himself to write confessions at all about his faith, there already lies a confession. Presumably, every one seems to have the right to compile an autobiography after his fortieth year; for the humblest amongst us may have experienced things, and may have seen them at such close quarters, that the recording of them may prove of use and value to the thinker. But to write a confession of one's faith cannot but be regarded as a thousand times more pretentious, since it takes for granted that the writer attaches worth, not only to the experiences and investigations of his life, but also to his beliefs. Now, what the nice thinker will require to know, above all else, is the kind of faith which happens to be compatible with natures of the Straussian order, and what it is they have "half dreamily conjured up" (p. 10) concerning matters of which those alone have the right to speak who are acquainted with them at first hand. Whoever would have desired to possess the confessions, say, of a Ranke or a Mommsen? And these men were scholars and historians of a very different stamp from David Strauss. If, however, they had ever ventured to interest us in their faith instead of in their scientific investigations, we should have felt that they were overstepping their limits in a most irritating fashion. Yet Strauss does this when he discusses his faith. Nobody wants to know anything about it, save, perhaps, a few bigoted opponents of the Straussian doctrines, who, suspecting, as they do, a substratum of satanic principles beneath these doctrines, hope that he may compromise his learned utterances by revealing the nature of those principles. These clumsy creatures may, perhaps, have found what they sought in the last book; but we, who had no occasion to suspect a satanic substratum, discovered nothing of the sort, and would have felt rather pleased than not had we been able to discern even a dash of the diabolical in any part of the volume. But surely no evil spirit could speak as Strauss speaks of his new faith. In fact, spirit in general seems to be altogether foreign to the book— more particularly the spirit of genius. Only those whom Strauss designates as his "We," speak as he does, and then, when they expatiate upon their faith to us, they bore us even more than when they relate their dreams; be they "scholars, artists, military men, civil employes, merchants, or landed proprietors; come they in their thousands, and not the worst people in the land either!" If they do not wish to remain the peaceful ones in town or county, but threaten to wax noisy, then let not the din of their *unisono* deceive us concerning the poverty and vulgarity of the melody they sing. How can it dispose us more favourably towards a profession of faith to hear that it is approved by a crowd, when it is of such an order that if any individual of that crowd attempted to make it known to us, we should not only fail to hear him out, but should interrupt him with a yawn? If thou sharest such a belief, we should say unto him, in Heaven's name, keep it to thyself! Maybe, in the past, some few harmless types looked for the thinker in David Strauss; now they have discovered the "believer" in him, and are disappointed. Had he kept silent, he would have remained, for these, at least, the philosopher; whereas, now, no one regards him as such. He no longer craved the honours of the thinker, however; all he wanted to be was a new believer, and he is proud of his new belief. In making a written declaration of it, he fancied he was writing the catechism of "modern thought," and building the "broad highway of the world's future." Indeed, our Philistines have ceased to be faint-hearted and bashful, and have acquired almost cynical assurance. There was a time, long, long ago, when the Philistine was only tolerated as something that did not speak, and about which no one spoke; then a period ensued during which his roughness was smoothed, during which he was found amusing, and people talked about him. Under this treatment he gradually became a prig, rejoiced with all his heart over his rough places and his wrongheaded and candid singularities, and began to talk, on his own account, after the style of Riehl's music for the home.

"But what do I see? Is it a shadow? Is it reality? How long and broad my poodle grows!"

For now he is already rolling like a hippopotamus along "the broad highway of the world's future," and his growling and barking have become transformed into the proud incantations of a religious founder. And is it your own sweet wish, Great Master, to found the religion of the future? "The times seem to us not yet ripe (p. 7). It does not occur to us to wish to destroy a church." But why not, Great Master? One but needs the ability. Besides, to speak quite openly in the latter, you yourself are convinced that you Possess this ability. Look at the last page of your book. There you actually state, forsooth, that your new way "alone is the future highway of the world, which now only requires partial completion, and especially general use, in order also to become easy and pleasant."

Make no further denials, then. The religious founder is unmasked, the convenient and agreeable highway leading to the Straussian Paradise is built. It is only the coach in which you wish to convey us that does not altogether satisfy you, unpretentious man that you are! You tell us in your concluding remarks: "Nor will I pretend that the coach to which my esteemed readers have been obliged to trust themselves with me fulfils every requirement,... all through one is much jolted" (p. 438). Ah! you are casting about for a compliment, you gallant old religious founder! But let us be straightforward with you. If your reader so regulates the perusal of the 368 pages of your religious catechism as to read only one page a day—that is to say, if he take it in the smallest possible doses-then, perhaps, we should be able to believe that he might suffer some evil effect from the book—if only as the outcome of his vexation when the results he expected fail to make themselves felt. Gulped down more heartily, however, and as much as possible being taken at each draught, according to the prescription to be recommended in the case of all modern books, the drink can work no mischief; and, after taking it, the reader will not necessarily be either out of sorts or out of temper, but rather merry and well-disposed, as though nothing had happened; as though no religion had been assailed, no world's highway been built, and no profession of faith been made. And I do indeed call this a result! The doctor, the drug, and the disease—everything forgotten! And the joyous laughter! The continual provocation to hilarity! You are to be envied, Sir; for you have founded the most attractive of all religions —one whose followers do honour to its founder by laughing at him.

IV.

The Philistine as founder of the religion of the future—that is the new belief in its most emphatic form of expression. The Philistine becomes a dreamer—that is the unheard-of occurrence which distinguishes the German nation of to-day. But for the present, in any case, let us maintain an attitude of caution towards this fantastic exaltation. For does not David Strauss himself advise us to exercise such caution, in the following profound passage, the general tone of which leads us to think of the Founder of Christianity rather than of our particular author? (p. 92): "We know there have been noble enthusiasts—enthusiasts of genius; the influence of an enthusiast can rouse, exalt, and produce prolonged historic effects; but we do not wish to choose him as the guide of our life. He will be sure to mislead us, if we do not subject his influence to the control of reason." But we know something more: we know that there are enthusiasts who are not intellectual, who do not rouse or exalt, and who, nevertheless, not only expect to be the guides of our lives, but, as such, to exercise a very lasting historical influence into the bargain, and to rule the future;—all the more reason why we should place their influence under the control of reason. Lichtenberg even said:

"There are enthusiasts quite devoid of ability, and these are really dangerous people." In the first place, as regards the above-mentioned control of reason, we should like to have candid answers to the three following questions: First, how does the new believer picture his heaven? Secondly, how far does the courage lent him by the new faith extend? And, thirdly, how does he write his books? Strauss the Confessor must answer the first and second questions; Strauss the Writer must answer the third.

The heaven of the new believer must, perforce, be a heaven upon earth; for the Christian "prospect of an immortal life in heaven," together with the other consolations, "must irretrievably vanish" for him who has but "one foot" on the Straussian platform. The way in which a religion represents its heaven is significant, and if it be true that Christianity knows no other heavenly occupations than singing and making music, the prospect of the Philistine, *à la* Strauss, is truly not a very comforting one. In the book of confessions, however, there is a page which treats of Paradise (p. 342). Happiest of Philistines, unroll this parchment scroll before anything else, and the whole of heaven will seem to clamber down to thee! "We would but indicate how we act, how we have acted these many years. Besides our profession—for we are members of the most various professions, and by no means exclusively consist of scholars or artists, but of military men and civil employes, of merchants and landed proprietors;... and again, as I have said already, there are not a few of us, but many thousands, and not the worst people in the country;—besides our profession, then, I say, we are eagerly accessible to all the higher interests of humanity; we have taken a vivid interest, during late years, and each after his manner has participated in the great national war, and the reconstruction of the German State; and we have been profoundly exalted by the turn events have taken, as unexpected as glorious, for our much tried nation. To the end of forming just conclusions in these things, we study history, which has now been made easy, even to the unlearned, by a series of attractively and popularly written works; at the same time, we endeavour to enlarge our knowledge of the natural sciences, where also there is no lack of sources of information; and lastly, in the writings of our great poets, in the performances of our great musicians, we find a stimulus for the intellect and heart, for wit and imagination, which leaves nothing to be desired. Thus we live, and hold on our way in joy."

"Here is our man!" cries the Philistine exultingly, who reads this: "for this is exactly how we live; it is indeed our daily life."* And how perfectly he understands the euphemism! When, for example, he refers to the historical studies by means of which we help ourselves in forming just conclusions regarding the political situation, what can he be thinking of, if it be not our newspaper-reading? When he speaks of the active part we take in the reconstruction of the German State, he surely has only our daily visits to the beer-garden in his mind; and is not a walk in the Zoological Gardens implied by 'the sources of information through which we endeavour to enlarge our knowledge of the natural sciences'? Finally, the theatres and concert-halls are referred to as places from which we take home 'a stimulus for wit and imagination which leaves nothing to be desired.'—With what dignity and wit he describes even the most suspicious of our doings! Here indeed is our man; for his heaven is our heaven!"

[Footnote * : This alludes to a German student-song.]

Thus cries the Philistine; and if we are not quite so satisfied as he, it is merely owing to the fact that we wanted to know more. Scaliger used to say: "What does it matter to us whether Montaigne drank red or white wine?" But, in this more important case, how greatly ought we to value definite particulars of this sort! If we could but learn how many pipes the Philistine smokes daily, according to the prescriptions of the new faith, and whether it is the *Spener* or the *National Gazette* that appeals to him over his coffee! But our curiosity is not satisfied. With regard to one point only do we receive more exhaustive information, and fortunately this point relates to the heaven in heaven—the private little art-rooms which will be consecrated to the use of great poets and musicians, and to which the Philistine will go to edify himself; in which, moreover, according to his own showing, he will even get "all his stains removed and wiped away" (p. 433); so that we are led to regard these private little art-rooms as a kind of bath-rooms. "But this is only effected for some fleeting moments; it happens and counts only in the realms of phantasy; as soon as we return to rude reality, and the cramping confines of actual life, we are again on all sides assailed by the old cares,"—thus our Master sighs. Let us, however, avail ourselves of the fleeting moments during which we remain in those little rooms; there is just sufficient time to get a glimpse of the apotheosis of the Philistine— that is to say, the Philistine whose stains have been removed and wiped away, and who is now an absolutely pure sample of his type. In truth, the opportunity we have here may prove instructive: let no one who happens to have fallen a victim to the confession-book lay it aside before having read the two appendices, "Of our Great Poets" and "Of our Great Musicians." Here the rainbow of the new brotherhood is set, and he who can find no pleasure in it "for such an one there is no help," as Strauss says on another occasion; and, as he might well say here, "he is not yet ripe for our point of view." For are we not in the heaven of heavens? The enthusiastic explorer undertakes to lead us about, and begs us to excuse him if, in the excess of his joy at all the beauties to be seen, he should by any chance be tempted to talk too much. "If I should, perhaps, become more garrulous than may seem warranted in this place, let the reader be indulgent to me; for out of the abundance of the heart the mouth speaketh. Let him only be assured that what he is now about to read does not consist of older materials, which I take the opportunity of inserting here, but that these remarks have been written for their present place and purpose" (pp. 345-46). This confession surprises us somewhat for the moment. What can it matter to us whether or not the little chapters were freshly written? As if it were a matter of writing! Between ourselves, I should have been glad if they had been written a quarter of a century earlier; then, at least, I should have understood why the thoughts seem to be so bleached, and why they are so redolent of resuscitated antiquities. But that a thing should have been written in 1872 and already smell of decay in 1872 strikes me as suspicious. Let us imagine some one's falling asleep while reading these chapters—what would he most probably dream about? A friend answered this question for me, because he happened to have had the experience himself. He dreamt of a wax-work show. The classical writers stood there, elegantly represented in wax and beads. Their arms and eyes moved, and a screw inside them creaked an accompaniment to their movements. He saw something gruesome among them—a misshapen figure, decked with tapes and jaundiced paper, out of whose mouth a ticket hung, on which "Lessing" was written. My friend went close up to it and learned the worst: it was the Homeric Chimera; in front it was Strauss, behind it was Gervinus, and in the middle Chimera. The *tout-ensemble* was Lessing. This discovery caused him to shriek with terror: he waked, and read no more. In sooth, Great Master, why have you written such fusty little chapters?

We do, indeed, learn something new from them; for instance, that Gervinus made it known to the world how and why Goethe was no dramatic genius; that, in the second part of Faust, he had only produced a world of phantoms and of symbols; that Wallenstein is a Macbeth as well as a Hamlet; that the Straussian reader extracts the short stories out of the *Wanderjahre* "much as naughty children pick the raisins and almonds out of a tough plum-cake"; that no complete effect can be produced on the stage without the forcible element, and that Schiller emerged from Kant as from a cold-water cure. All this is certainly new and striking; but, even so, it does not strike us with wonder, and so sure as it is new, it will never grow old, for it never was young; it was senile at birth. What extraordinary ideas seem to occur to these Blessed Ones, after the New Style, in their aesthetic heaven! And why can they not manage to forget a few of them, more particularly when they are of that unaesthetic, earthly, and ephemeral order to which the scholarly thoughts of Gervinus belong, and when they so obviously bear the stamp of puerility? But it almost seems as though the modest greatness of a Strauss and the vain insignificance of a Gervinus were only too well able to harmonise: then long live all those Blessed Ones! may we, the rejected, also live long, if this unchallenged judge of art continues any longer to teach his borrowed enthusiasm, and the gallop of that hired steed of which the honest Grillparzer speaks with such delightful clearness, until the whole of heaven rings beneath the hoof of that galumphing enthusiasm. Then, at least, things will be livelier and noisier than they are at the present moment, in which the carpet-slippered rapture of our heavenly leader and the lukewarm eloquence of his lips only succeed in the end in making us sick and tired. I should like to know how a Hallelujah sung by Strauss would sound: I believe one would have to listen very carefully, lest it should seem no more than a courteous apology or a lisped compliment. Apropos of this, I might adduce an instructive and somewhat forbidding example. Strauss strongly resented the action of one of his opponents who happened to refer to his reverence for Lessing. The unfortunate man had misunderstood;—true, Strauss did declare that one must be of a very obtuse mind not to recognise that the simple words of paragraph 86 come from the writer's heart. Now, I do not question this warmth in the very least; on the contrary, the fact that Strauss fosters these feelings towards Lessing has always excited my suspicion; I find the same warmth for Lessing raised almost to heat in Gervinus—yea, on the whole, no great German writer is so popular among little German writers as Lessing is; but for all that, they deserve no thanks for their predilection; for what is it, in sooth, that they praise in Lessing? At one moment it is his catholicity— the fact that he was critic and poet, archaeologist and philosopher, dramatist and theologian. Anon, "it is the unity in him of the writer and the man, of the head and the heart." The last quality, as a rule, is just as characteristic of the great writer as of the little one; as a rule, a narrow head agrees only too fatally with a narrow heart. And as to the catholicity; this is no distinction, more especially when, as in Lessing's case, it was a dire necessity. What astonishes one in regard to Lessing-enthusiasts is rather that they have no conception of the devouring necessity which drove him on through life and to this catholicity; no feeling for the fact that such a man is too prone to consume himself rapidly, like a flame; nor any indignation at the thought that the vulgar narrowness and pusillanimity of his whole environment, especially of his learned contemporaries, so saddened, tormented, and stifled the tender and ardent creature that he was, that the very universality for which he is praised should give rise to feelings of the deepest compassion. "Have pity on the exceptional man!" Goethe cries to us; "for it was his lot to live in such a wretched age that his life was one long polemical effort." How can ye, my worthy Philistines, think of Lessing without shame? He who was ruined precisely on account of your stupidity, while struggling with your ludicrous fetiches and idols, with the defects of your theatres, scholars, and theologists, without once daring to attempt that eternal flight for which he had been born. And what are your feelings when ye think of Winckelman, who, in order to turn his eyes from your grotesque puerilities, went begging to the Jesuits for help, and whose ignominious conversion dishonours not him, but you? Dare ye mention Schiller's name without blushing? Look at his portrait. See the flashing eyes that glance contemptuously over your heads, the deadly red cheek—do these things mean nothing to you? In him ye had such a magnificent and divine toy that ye shattered it. Suppose, for a moment, it had been possible to deprive this harassed and hunted life of Goethe's friendship, ye would then have been reponsible for its still earlier end. Ye have had no finger in any one of the life-works of your great geniuses, and yet ye would make a dogma to the effect that no one is to be helped in the future. But for every one of them, ye were "the resistance of the obtuse world," which Goethe calls by its name in his epilogue to the Bell; for all of them ye were the grumbling imbeciles, or the envious bigots, or the malicious egoists: in spite of you each of them created his works, against you each directed his attacks, and thanks to you each prematurely sank, while his work was still unfinished, broken and bewildered by the stress of the battle. And now ye presume that ye are going to be permitted, *tamquam re bene gesta*, to praise such men! and with words which leave no one in any doubt as to whom ye have in your minds when ye utter your encomiums, which therefore "spring forth with such hearty warmth" that one must be blind not to see to whom ye are really bowing. Even Goethe in his day had to cry: "Upon my honour, we are in need of a Lessing, and woe unto all vain masters and to the whole aesthetic kingdom of heaven, when the young tiger, whose restless strength will be visible in his every distended muscle and his every glance, shall sally forth to seek his prey!"

V.

How clever it was of my friend to read no further, once he had been enlightened (thanks to that chimerical vision) concerning the Straussian Lessing and Strauss himself. We, however, read on further, and even craved admission of the Doorkeeper of the New Faith to the sanctum of music. The Master threw the door open for us, accompanied us, and began quoting certain names, until, at last, overcome with mistrust, we stood still and looked at him. Was it possible that we were the victims of the same hallucination as that to which our friend had been subjected in his dream? The musicians to whom Strauss referred seemed to us to be wrongly designated as long as he spoke about them, and we began to think that the talk must certainly be about somebody else, even admitting that it did not relate to incongruous phantoms. When, for instance, he mentioned Haydn with that same warmth which made us so suspicious when he praised Lessing, and when he posed as the epopt and priest of a mysterious Haydn cult; when, in a discussion upon quartette-music, if you please, he even likened Haydn to a "good unpretending soup" and Beethoven to "sweetmeats" (p. 432); then, to our minds, one thing, and one thing alone, became certain—namely, that his Sweetmeat-Beethoven is not our Beethoven, and his Soup-Haydn is not our Haydn. The Master was moreover of the opinion that our orchestra is too good to perform Haydn, and that only the most unpretentious amateurs can do justice to that music—a further proof that he was referring to some other artist and some other work, possibly to Riehl's music for the home.

But whoever can this Sweetmeat-Beethoven of Strauss's be? He is said to have composed nine symphonies, of which the Pastoral is "the least remarkable"; we are told that "each time in composing the third, he seemed impelled to exceed his bounds, and depart on an adventurous quest," from which we might infer that we are here concerned with a sort of double monster, half horse and half cavalier. With regard to a certain *Eroica*, this Centaur is very hard pressed, because he did not succeed in making it clear "whether it is a question of a conflict on the open field or in the deep heart of man." In the Pastoral there is said to be "a furiously raging storm," for which it is "almost too insignificant" to interrupt a dance of country-folk, and which, owing to "its arbitrary connection with a trivial motive," as Strauss so adroitly and correctly puts it, renders this symphony "the least remarkable." A more drastic expression appears to have occurred to the Master; but he prefers to speak here, as he says, "with becoming modesty." But no, for once our Master is wrong; in this case he is really a little too modest. Who, indeed, will enlighten us concerning this Sweetmeat-Beethoven, if not Strauss himself—the only person who seems to know anything about him? But, immediately below, a strong judgment is uttered with becoming non-modesty, and precisely in regard to the Ninth Symphony. It is said, for instance, that this symphony "is naturally the favourite of a prevalent taste, which in art, and music especially, mistakes the grotesque for the genial, and the formless for the sublime" (p. 428). It is true that a critic as severe as Gervinus was gave this work a hearty welcome, because it happened to confirm one of his doctrines; but Strauss is "far from going to these problematic productions" in search of the merits of his Beethoven. "It is a pity," cries our Master, with a convulsive sigh, "that one is compelled, by such reservations, to mar one's enjoyment of Beethoven, as well as the admiration gladly accorded to him." For our Master is a favourite of the Graces, and these have informed him that they only accompanied Beethoven part of the way, and that he then lost sight of them. "This is a defect," he cries, "but can you believe that it may also appear as an advantage?" "He who is painfully and breathlessly rolling the musical idea along will seem to be moving the weightier one, and thus appear to be the stronger" (pp. 423-24). This is a confession, and not necessarily one concerning Beethoven alone, but concerning "the classical prose-writer" himself. He, the celebrated author, is not abandoned by the Graces. From the play of airy jests—that is to say, Straussian jests— to the heights of solemn earnestness—that is to say, Straussian earnestness—they remain stolidly at his elbow. He, the classical prose-writer, slides his burden along playfully and with a light heart, whereas Beethoven rolls his painfully and breathlessly. He seems merely to dandle his load; this is indeed an advantage. But would anybody believe that it might equally be a sign of something wanting? In any case, only those could believe this who mistake the grotesque for the genial, and the formless for the sublime—is not that so, you dandling favourite of the Graces? We envy no one the edifying moments he may have, either in the stillness of his little private room or in a new heaven specially fitted out for him; but of all possible pleasures of this order, that of Strauss's is surely one of the most wonderful, for he is even edified by a little holocaust. He calmly throws the sublimest works of the German nation into the flames, in order to cense his idols with their smoke. Suppose, for a moment, that by some accident, the Eroica, the Pastoral, and the Ninth Symphony had fallen into the hands of our priest of the Graces, and that it had been in his power to suppress such problematic productions, in order to keep the image of the Master pure, who doubts but what he would have burned them? And it is precisely in this way that the Strausses of our time demean themselves: they only wish to know so much of an artist as is compatible with the service of their rooms; they know only the extremes— censing or burning. To all this they are heartily welcome; the one surprising feature of the whole case is that public opinion, in matters artistic, should be so feeble, vacillating, and corruptible as contentedly to allow these exhibitions of indigent Philistinism to go by without raising an objection; yea, that it does not even possess sufficient sense of humour to feel tickled at the sight of an unaesthetic little master's sitting in judgment upon Beethoven. As to Mozart, what Aristotle says of Plato ought really to be applied here: "Insignificant people ought not to be permitted even to praise him." In this respect, however, all shame has vanished—from the public as well as from the Master's mind: he is allowed, not merely to cross himself before the greatest and purest creations of German genius, as though he had perceived something godless and immoral in them, but people actually rejoice over his candid confessions and admission of sins—more particularly as he makes no mention of his own, but only of those which great men are said to have committed. Oh, if only our Master be in the right! his readers sometimes think, when attacked by a paroxysm of doubt; he himself, however, stands there, smiling and convinced, perorating, condemning, blessing, raising his hat to himself, and is at any minute capable of saying what the Duchesse Delaforte said to Madame de Staël, to wit: "My dear, I must confess that I find no one but myself invariably right."

VI.

A corpse is a pleasant thought for a worm, and a worm is a dreadful thought for every living creature. Worms fancy their kingdom of heaven in a fat body; professors of philosophy seek theirs in rummaging among Schopenhauer's entrails, and as long as rodents exist, there will exist a heaven for rodents. In this, we have the answer to our first question: How does the believer in the new faith picture his heaven? The Straussian Philistine harbours in the works of our great poets and musicians like a parasitic worm whose life is destruction, whose admiration is devouring, and whose worship is digesting.

Now, however, our second question must be answered: How far does the courage lent to its adherents by this new faith extend? Even this question would already have been answered, if courage and pretentiousness had been one; for then Strauss would not be lacking even in the just and veritable courage of a Mameluke. At all events, the "becoming modesty" of which Strauss speaks in the above-mentioned passage, where he is referring to Beethoven, can only be a stylistic and not a moral manner of speech. Strauss has his full share of the temerity to which every successful hero assumes the right: all flowers grow only for him—the conqueror; and he praises the sun because it shines in at his window just at the right time. He does not even spare the venerable old universe in his eulogies—as though it were only now and henceforward sufficiently sanctified by praise to revolve around the central monad David Strauss. The universe, he is happy to inform us, is, it is true, a machine with jagged iron wheels, stamping and hammering ponderously, but: "We do not only find the revolution of pitiless wheels in our world-machine, but also the shedding of soothing oil" (p. 435). The universe, provided it submit to Strauss's encomiums, is not likely to overflow with gratitude towards this master of weird metaphors, who was unable to discover better similes in its praise. But what is the oil called which trickles down upon the hammers and stampers? And how would it console a workman who chanced to get one of his limbs caught in the mechanism to know that this oil was trickling over him? Passing over this simile as bad, let us turn our attention to another of Strauss's artifices, whereby he tries to ascertain how he feels disposed towards the universe; this question of Marguerite's, "He loves me—loves me not—loves me?" hanging on his lips the while. Now, although Strauss is not telling flower-petals or the buttons on his waistcoat, still what he does is not less harmless, despite the fact that it needs perhaps a little more courage. Strauss wishes to make certain whether his feeling for the "All" is either paralysed or withered, and he pricks himself; for he knows that one can prick a limb that is either paralysed or withered without causing any pain. As a matter of fact, he does not really prick himself, but selects another more violent method, which he describes thus: "We open Schopenhauer, who takes every occasion of slapping our idea in the face" (p. 167). Now, as an idea—even that of Strauss's concerning the universe—has no face, if there be any face in the question at all it must be that of the idealist, and the procedure may be subdivided into the following separate actions:—Strauss, in any case, throws Schopenhauer open, whereupon the latter slaps Strauss in the face. Strauss then reacts religiously; that is to say, he again begins to belabour Schopenhauer, to abuse him, to speak of absurdities, blasphemies, dissipations, and even to allege that Schopenhauer could not have been in his right senses. Result of the dispute: "We demand the same piety for our Cosmos that the devout of old demanded for his God"; or, briefly, "He loves me." Our favourite of the Graces makes his life a hard one, but he is as brave as a Mameluke, and fears neither the Devil nor Schopenhauer. How much "soothing oil" must he use if such incidents are of frequent occurrence!

On the other hand, we readily understand Strauss's gratitude to this tickling, pricking, and slapping Schopenhauer; hence we are not so very much surprised when we find him expressing himself in the following kind way about him: "We need only turn over the leaves of Arthur Schopenhauer's works (although we shall on many other accounts do well not only to glance over but to study them), etc." (p. 166). Now, to whom does this captain of Philistines address these words? To him who has clearly never even studied Schopenhauer, the latter might well have retorted, "This is an author who does not even deserve to be scanned, much less to be studied." Obviously, he gulped Schopenhauer down "the wrong way," and this hoarse coughing is merely his attempt to clear his throat. But, in order to fill the measure of his ingenuous encomiums, Strauss even arrogates to himself the right of commending old Kant: he speaks of the latter's *General History of the Heavens of the Year 1755* as of "a work which has always appeared to me not less important than his later *Critique of Pure Reason*. If in the latter we admire the depth of insight, the breadth of observation strikes us in the former. If in the latter we can trace the old man's anxiety to secure even a limited possession of knowledge—so it be but on a firm basis—in the former we encounter the mature man, full of the daring of the discoverer and conqueror in the realm of thought." This judgment of Strauss's concerning Kant did not strike me as being more modest than the one concerning Schopenhauer. In the one case, we have the little captain, who is above all anxious to express even the most insignificant opinion with certainty, and in the other we have the famous prose-writer, who, with all the courage of ignorance, exudes his eulogistic secretions over Kant. It is almost incredible that Strauss availed himself of nothing in Kant's *Critique of Pure Reason* while compiling his Testament of modern ideas, and that he knew only how to appeal to the coarsest realistic taste must also be numbered among the more striking characteristics of this new gospel, the which professes to be but the result of the laborious and continuous study of history and science, and therefore tacitly repudiates all connection with philosophy. For the Philistine captain and his "We," Kantian philosophy does not exist. He does not dream of the fundamental antinomy of idealism and of the highly relative sense of all science and reason. And it is precisely reason that ought to tell him how little it is possible to know of things in themselves. It is true, however, that people of a certain age cannot possibly understand Kant, especially when, in their youth, they understood or fancied they understood that "gigantic mind," Hegel, as Strauss did; and had moreover concerned themselves with Schleiermacher, who, according to Strauss, "was gifted with perhaps too much acumen." It will sound odd to our author when I tell him that, even now, he stands absolutely dependent upon Hegel and Schleiermacher, and that his teaching of the Cosmos, his way of regarding things *sub specie biennii*, his salaams to the state of affairs now existing in Germany, and, above all, his shameless Philistine optimism, can only be explained by an appeal to certain impressions of youth, early habits, and disorders; for he who has once sickened on Hegel and Schleiermacher never completely recovers.

There is one passage in the confession-book where the incurable optimism referred to above bursts forth with the full joyousness of holiday spirits (pp. 166-67). "If the universe is a thing which had better not have existed," says Strauss, "then surely the speculation of the philosopher, as forming part of this universe, is a speculation which had better not have speculated. The pessimist philosopher fails to perceive that he, above all, declares his own thought, which declares the world to be bad, as bad also; but if the thought which declares the world to be bad is a bad thought, then it follows naturally that the world is good. As a rule, optimism may take things too easily. Schopenhauer's references to the colossal part which sorrow and evil play in the world are quite in their right place as a counterpoise; but every true philosophy is necessarily optimistic, as otherwise she hews down the branch on which she herself is sitting." If this refutation of Schopenhauer is not the same as that to which Strauss refers somewhere else as "the refutation loudly and jubilantly acclaimed in higher spheres," then I quite fail to understand the dramatic phraseology used by him elsewhere to strike an opponent. Here optimism has for once intentionally simplified her task. But the master-stroke lay in thus pretending that the refutation of Schopenhauer was not such a very difficult task after all, and in playfully wielding the burden in such a manner that the three Graces attendant on the dandling optimist might constantly be delighted by his methods. The whole purpose of the deed was to demonstrate this one truth, that it is quite unnecessary to take a pessimist seriously; the most vapid sophisms become justified, provided they show that, in regard to a philosophy as "unhealthy and unprofitable" as Schopenhauer's, not proofs but quips and sallies alone are suitable. While perusing such passages, the reader will grasp the full meaning of Schopenhauer's solemn utterance to the effect that, where optimism is not merely the idle prattle of those beneath whose flat brows words and only words are stored, it seemed to him not merely an absurd *but a vicious attitude of mind*, and one full of scornful irony towards the indescribable sufferings of humanity. When a philosopher like Strauss is able to frame it into a system, it becomes more than a vicious attitude of mind—it is then an imbecile gospel of comfort for the "I" or for the "We," and can only provoke indignation.

Who could read the following psychological avowal, for instance, without indignation, seeing that it is obviously but an offshoot from this vicious gospel of comfort?—"Beethoven remarked that he could never have composed a text like Figaro or Don Juan. *Life had not been so profuse of its snubs to him that he could treat it so gaily, or deal so lightly with the foibles of men*" (p. 430). In order, however, to adduce the most striking instance of this dissolute vulgarity of sentiment, let it suffice, here, to observe that Strauss knows no other means of accounting for the terribly serious negative instinct and the movement of ascetic sanctification which characterised the first century of the Christian era, than by supposing the existence of a previous period of surfeit in the matter of all kinds of sexual indulgence, which of itself brought about a state of revulsion and disgust.

"The Persians call it *bidamag buden*, The Germans say '*Katzenjammer*.'"*

] [Footnote * : Remorse for the previous night's excesses.—Translator's note.

Strauss quotes this himself, and is not ashamed. As for us, we turn aside for a moment, that we may overcome our loathing.

VII.

As a matter of fact, our Philistine captain is brave, even audacious, in words; particularly when he hopes by such bravery to delight his noble colleagues— the "We," as he calls them. So the asceticism and self-denial of the ancient anchorite and saint was merely a form of *Katzenjammer*? Jesus may be described as an enthusiast who nowadays would scarcely have escaped the madhouse, and the story of the Resurrection may be termed a "world-wide deception." For once we will allow these views to pass without raising any objection, seeing that they may help us to gauge the amount of courage which our "classical Philistine" Strauss is capable of. Let us first hear his confession: "It is certainly an unpleasant and a thankless task to tell the world those truths which it is least desirous of hearing. It prefers, in fact, to manage its affairs on a profuse scale, receiving and spending after the magnificent fashion of the great, as long as there is anything left; should any person, however, add up the various items of its liabilities, and anxiously call its attention to the sum-total, he is certain to be regarded as an importunate meddler. And yet this has always been the bent of my moral and intellectual nature." A moral and intellectual nature of this sort might possibly be regarded as courageous; but what still remains to be proved is, whether this courage is natural and inborn, or whether it is not rather acquired and artificial. Perhaps Strauss only accustomed himself by degrees to the rôle of an importunate meddler, until he gradually acquired the courage of his calling. Innate cowardice, which is the Philistine's birthright, would not be incompatible with this mode of development, and it is precisely this cowardice which is perceptible in the want of logic of those sentences of Strauss's which it needed courage to pronounce. They sound like thunder, but they do not clear the air. No aggressive action is performed: aggressive words alone are used, and these he selects from among the most insulting he can find. He moreover exhausts all his accumulated strength and energy in coarse and noisy expression, and when once his utterances have died away he is more of a coward even than he who has always held his tongue. The very shadow of his deeds—his morality—shows us that he is a word-hero, and that he avoids everything which might induce him to transfer his energies from mere verbosity to really serious things. With admirable frankness, he announces that he is no longer a Christian, but disclaims all idea of wishing to disturb the contentment of any one: he seems to recognise a contradiction in the notion of abolishing one society by instituting another—whereas there is nothing contradictory in it at all. With a certain rude self-satisfaction, he swathes himself in the hirsute garment of our Simian genealogists, and extols Darwin as one of mankind's greatest benefactors; but our perplexity is great when we find him constructing his ethics quite independently of the question, "What is our conception of the universe?" In this department he had an opportunity of exhibiting native pluck; for he ought to have turned his back on his "We," and have established a moral code for life out of *bellum omnium contra omnes* and the privileges of the strong. But it is to be feared that such a code could only have emanated from a bold spirit like that of Hobbes', and must have taken its root in a love of truth quite different from that which was only able to vent itself in explosive outbursts against parsons, miracles, and the "world-wide humbug" of the Resurrection. For, whereas the Philistine remained on Strauss's side in regard to these explosive outbursts, he would have been against him had he been confronted with a genuine and seriously constructed ethical system, based upon Darwin's teaching.

Says Strauss: "I should say that all moral action arises from the individual's acting in consonance with the idea of kind" (p. 274). Put quite clearly and comprehensively, this means: "Live as a man, and not as an ape or a seal." Unfortunately, this imperative is both useless and feeble; for in the class *Man* what a multitude of different types are included—to mention only the Patagonian and the Master, Strauss; and no one would ever dare to say with any right, "Live like a Patagonian," and "Live like the Master Strauss"! Should any one, however, make it his rule to live like a genius—that is to say, like the ideal type of the genus Man—and should he perchance at the same time be either a Patagonian or Strauss himself, what should we then not have to suffer from the importunities of genius-mad eccentrics (concerning whose mushroom growth in Germany even Lichtenberg had already spoken), who with savage cries would compel us to listen to the confession of their most recent belief! Strauss has not yet learned that no "idea" can ever make man better or more moral, and that the preaching of a morality is as easy as the establishment of it is difficult. His business ought rather to have been, to take the phenomena of human goodness, such—for instance—as pity, love, and self-abnegation, which are already to hand, and seriously to explain them and show their relation to his Darwinian first principle. But no; he preferred to soar into the imperative, and thus escape the task of explaining. But even in his flight he was irresponsible enough to soar beyond the very first principles of which we speak.

"Ever remember," says Strauss, "that thou art human, not merely a natural production; ever remember that all others are human also, and, with all individual differences, the same as thou, having the same needs and claims as thyself: this is the sum and the substance of morality" (p. 277). But where does this imperative hail from? How can it be intuitive in man, seeing that, according to Darwin, man is indeed a creature of nature, and that his ascent to his present stage of development has been conditioned by quite different laws—by the very fact that be was continually forgetting that others were constituted like him and shared the same rights with him; by the very fact that he regarded himself as the stronger, and thus brought about the gradual suppression of weaker types. Though Strauss is bound to admit that no two creatures have ever been quite alike, and that the ascent of man from the lowest species of animals to the exalted height of the Culture—Philistine depended upon the law of individual distinctness, he still sees no difficulty in declaring exactly the reverse in his law: "Behave thyself as though there were no such things as individual distinctions." Where is the Strauss-Darwin morality here? Whither, above all, has the courage gone?

In the very next paragraph we find further evidence tending to show us the point at which this courage veers round to its opposite; for Strauss continues: "Ever remember that thou, and all that thou beholdest within and around thee, all that befalls thee and others, is no disjointed fragment, no wild chaos of atoms or casualties, but that, following eternal law, it springs from the one primal source of all life, all reason, and all good: this is the essence of religion" (pp. 277-78). Out of that "one primal source," however, all ruin and irrationality, all evil flows as well, and its name, according to Strauss, is Cosmos.

Now, how can this Cosmos, with all the contradictions and the self-annihilating characteristics which Strauss gives it, be worthy of religious veneration and be addressed by the name "God," as Strauss addresses it?— "Our God does not, indeed, take us into His arms from the outside (here one expects, as an antithesis, a somewhat miraculous process of being "taken into His arms from the inside"), but He unseals the well-springs of consolation within our own bosoms. He shows us that although Chance would be an unreasonable ruler, yet necessity, or the enchainment of causes in the world, is Reason itself." (A misapprehension of which only the "We" can fail to perceive the folly; because they were brought up in the Hegelian worship of Reality as the Reasonable—that is to say, in the canonisation of success.) "He teaches us to perceive that to demand an exception in the accomplishment of a single natural law would be to demand the destruction of the universe" (pp. 435-36). On the contrary, Great Master: an honest natural scientist believes in the unconditional rule of natural laws in the world, without, however, taking up any position in regard to the ethical or intellectual value of these laws. Wherever neutrality is abandoned in this respect, it is owing to an anthropomorphic attitude of mind which allows reason to exceed its proper bounds. But it is just at the point where the natural scientist resigns that Strauss, to put it in his own words, "reacts religiously," and leaves the scientific and scholarly standpoint in order to proceed along less honest lines of his own. Without any further warrant, he assumes that all that has happened possesses the highest intellectual value; that it was therefore absolutely reasonably and intentionally so arranged, and that it even contained a revelation of eternal goodness. He therefore has to appeal to a complete cosmodicy, and finds himself at a disadvantage in regard to him who is contented with a theodicy, and who, for instance, regards the whole of man's existence as a punishment for sin or a process of purification. At this stage, and in this embarrassing position, Strauss even suggests a metaphysical hypothesis—the driest and most palsied ever conceived—and, in reality, but an unconscious parody of one of Lessing's sayings. We read on page 255: "And that other saying of Lessing's— 'If God, holding truth in His right hand, and in His left only the ever-living desire for it, although on condition of perpetual error, left him the choice of the two, he would, considering that truth belongs to God alone, humbly seize His left hand, and beg its contents for Himself'— this saying of Lessing's has always been accounted one of the most magnificent which he has left us. It has been found to contain the general expression of his restless love of inquiry and activity. The saying has always made a special impression upon me; because, behind its subjective meaning, I still seemed to hear the faint ring of an objective one of infinite import. For does it not contain the best possible answer to the rude speech of Schopenhauer, respecting the ill-advised God who had nothing better to do than to transform Himself into this miserable world? if, for example, the Creator Himself had shared Lessing's conviction of the superiority of struggle to tranquil possession?" What!—a God who would choose *perpetual error*, together with a striving after truth, and who would, perhaps, fall humbly at Strauss's feet and cry to him,"Take thou all Truth, it is thine!"? If ever a God and a man were ill-advised, they are this

Straussian God, whose hobby is to err and to fail, and this Straussian man, who must atone for this erring and failing. Here, indeed, one hears "a faint ring of infinite import"; here flows Strauss's cosmic soothing oil; here one has a notion of the *rationale* of all becoming and all natural laws. Really? Is not our universe rather the work of an inferior being, as Lichtenberg suggests?—of an inferior being who did not quite understand his business; therefore an experiment, an attempt, upon which work is still proceeding? Strauss himself, then, would be compelled to admit that our universe is by no means the theatre of reason, but of error, and that no conformity to law can contain anything consoling, since all laws have been promulgated by an erratic God who even finds pleasure in blundering. It really is a most amusing spectacle to watch Strauss as a metaphysical architect, building castles in the air. But for whose benefit is this entertainment given? For the smug and noble "We," that they may not lose conceit with themselves: they may possibly have taken sudden fright, in the midst of the inflexible and pitiless wheel-works of the world-machine, and are tremulously imploring their leader to come to their aid. That is why Strauss pours forth the "soothing oil," that is why he leads forth on a leash a God whose passion it is to err; it is for the same reason, too, that he assumes for once the utterly unsuitable rôle of a metaphysical architect. He does all this, because the noble souls already referred to are frightened, and because he is too. And it is here that we reach the limit of his courage, even in the presence of his "We." He does not dare to be honest, and to tell them, for instance: "I have liberated you from a helping and pitiful God: the Cosmos is no more than an inflexible machine; beware of its wheels, that they do not crush you." He dare not do this. Consequently, he must enlist the help of a witch, and he turns to metaphysics. To the Philistine, however, even Strauss's metaphysics is preferable to Christianity's, and the notion of an erratic God more congenial than that of one who works miracles. For the Philistine himself errs, but has never yet performed a miracle. Hence his hatred of the genius; for the latter is justly famous for the working of miracles. It is therefore highly instructive to ascertain why Strauss, in one passage alone, suddenly takes up the cudgels for genius and the aristocracy of intellect in general. Whatever does he do it for? He does it out of fear—fear of the social democrat. He refers to Bismarck and Moltke, "whose greatness is the less open to controversy as it manifests itself in the domain of tangible external facts. No help for it, therefore; even the most stiff-necked and obdurate of these fellows must condescend to look up a little, if only to get a sight, be it no farther than the knees, of those august figures" (p.327). Do you, Master Metaphysician, perhaps intend to instruct the social democrats in the art of getting kicks? The willingness to bestow them may be met with everywhere, and you are perfectly justified in promising to those who happen to be kicked a sight of those sublime beings as far as the knee. "Also in the domain of art and science," Strauss continues, "there will never be a dearth of kings whose architectural undertakings will find employment for a multitude of carters." Granted; but what if the carters should begin building? It does happen at times, Great Master, as you know, and then the kings must grin and bear it.

As a matter of fact, this union of impudence and weakness, of daring words and cowardly concessions, this cautious deliberation as to which sentences will or will not impress the Philistine or smooth him down the right way, this lack of character and power masquerading as character and power, this meagre wisdom in the guise of omniscience,—these are the features in this book which I detest. If I could conceive of young men having patience to read it and to value it, I should sorrowfully renounce all hope for their future. And is this confession of wretched, hopeless, and really despicable Philistinism supposed to be the expression of the thousands constituting the "We" of whom Strauss speaks, and who are to be the fathers of the coming generation? Unto him who would fain help this coming generation to acquire what the present one does not yet possess, namely, a genuine German culture, the prospect is a horrible one. To such a man, the ground seems strewn with ashes, and all stars are obscured; while every withered tree and field laid waste seems to cry to him: Barren! Forsaken! Springtime is no longer possible here! He must feel as young Goethe felt when he first peered into the melancholy atheistic twilight of the *Système de la Nature*; to him this book seemed so grey, so Cimmerian and deadly, that he could only endure its presence with difficulty, and shuddered at it as one shudders at a spectre.

VIII.

We ought now to be sufficiently informed concerning the heaven and the courage of our new believer to be able to turn to the last question: How does he write his books? and of what order are his religious documents?

He who can answer this question uprightly and without prejudice will be confronted by yet another serious problem, and that is: How this Straussian pocket-oracle of the German Philistine was able to pass through six editions? And he will grow more than ever suspicious when he hears that it was actually welcomed as a pocket-oracle, not only in scholastic circles, but even in German universities as well. Students are said to have greeted it as a canon for strong intellects, and, from all accounts, the professors raised no objections to this view; while here and there people have declared it to be a *religions book for scholars*. Strauss himself gave out that he did not intend his profession of faith to be merely a reference-book for learned and cultured people; but here let us abide by the fact that it was first and foremost a work appealing to his colleagues, and was ostensibly a mirror in which they were to see their own way of living faithfully reflected. For therein lay the feat. The Master feigned to have presented us with a new ideal conception of the universe, and now adulation is being paid him out of every mouth; because each is in a position to suppose that he too regards the universe and life in the same way. Thus Strauss has seen fulfilled in each of his readers what he only demanded of the future. In this way, the extraordinary success of his book is partly explained: "Thus we live and hold on our way in joy," the scholar cries in his book, and delights to see others rejoicing over the announcement. If the reader happen to think differently from the Master in regard to Darwin or to capital punishment, it is of very little consequence; for he is too conscious throughout of breathing an atmosphere that is familiar to him, and of hearing but the echoes of his own voice and wants. However painfully this unanimity may strike the true friend of German culture, it is his duty to be unrelenting in his explanation of it as a phenomenon, and not to shrink from making this explanation public.

We all know the peculiar methods adopted in our own time of cultivating the sciences: we all know them, because they form a part of our lives. And, for this very reason, scarcely anybody seems to ask himself what the result of such a cultivation of the sciences will mean to culture in general, even supposing that everywhere the highest abilities and the most earnest will be available for the promotion of culture. In the heart of the average scientific type (quite irrespective of the examples thereof with which we meet to-day) there lies a pure paradox: he behaves like the veriest idler of independent means, to whom life is not a dreadful and serious business, but a sound piece of property, settled upon him for all eternity; and it seems to him justifiable to spend his whole life in answering questions which, after all is said and done, can only be of interest to that person who believes in eternal life as an absolute certainty. The heir of but a few hours, he sees himself encompassed by yawning abysses, terrible to behold; and every step he takes should recall the questions, Wherefore? Whither? and Whence? to his mind. But his soul rather warms to his work, and, be this the counting of a floweret's petals or the breaking of stones by the roadside, he spends his whole fund of interest, pleasure, strength, and aspirations upon it. This paradox—the scientific man—has lately dashed ahead at such a frantic speed in Germany, that one would almost think the scientific world were a factory, in which every minute wasted meant a fine. To-day the man of science works as arduously as the fourth or slave caste: his study has ceased to be an occupation, it is a necessity; he looks neither to the right nor to the left, but rushes through all things—even through the serious matters which life bears in its train—with that semi-listlessness and repulsive need of rest so characteristic of the exhausted labourer. *This is also his attitude towards culture.* He behaves as if life to him were not only *otium* but *sine dignitate*: even in his sleep he does not throw off the yoke, but like an emancipated slave still dreams of his misery, his forced haste and his floggings. Our scholars can scarcely be distinguished—and, even then, not to their advantage—from agricultural labourers, who in order to increase a small patrimony, assiduously strive, day and night, to cultivate their fields, drive their ploughs, and urge on their oxen. Now, Pascal suggests that men only endeavour to work hard at their business and sciences with the view of escaping those questions of greatest import which every moment of loneliness or leisure presses upon them—the questions relating to the *wherefore*, the *whence*, and the *whither* of life. Curiously enough, our scholars never think of the most vital question of all—the wherefore of their work, their haste, and their painful ecstasies. Surely their object is not the earning of bread or the acquiring of posts of honour? No, certainly not. But ye take as much pains as the famishing and breadless; and, with that eagerness and lack of discernment which characterises the starving, ye even snatch the dishes from the sideboard of science. If, however, as scientific men, ye proceed with science as the labourers with the tasks which the exigencies of life impose upon them, what will become of a culture which must await the hour of its birth and its salvation in the very midst of all this agitated and breathless running to and fro—this sprawling scientifically?

For *it* no one has time—and yet for what shall science have time if not for culture? Answer us here, then, at least: whence, whither, wherefore all science, if it do not lead to culture? Belike to barbarity? And in this direction we already see the scholar caste ominously advanced, if we are to believe that such superficial books as this one of Strauss's meet the demand of their present degree of culture. For precisely in him do we find that repulsive need of rest and that incidental semi-listless attention to, and coming to terms with, philosophy, culture, and every serious thing on earth. It will be remembered that, at the meetings held by scholars, as soon as each individual has had his say in his own particular department of knowledge, signs of fatigue, of a desire for distraction at any price, of waning memory, and of incoherent experiences of life, begin to be noticeable. While listening to Strauss discussing any worldly question, be it marriage, the war, or capital punishment, we are startled by his complete lack of anything like first-hand experience, or of any original thought on human nature. All his judgments are so redolent of books, yea even of newspapers. Literary reminiscences do duty for genuine ideas and views, and the assumption of a moderate and grandfatherly tone take the place of wisdom and mature thought. How perfectly in keeping all this is with the fulsome spirit animating the holders of the highest places in German science in large cities! How thoroughly this spirit must appeal to that other! for it is precisely in those quarters that culture is in the saddest plight; it is precisely there that its fresh growth is made impossible—so boisterous are the preparations made by science, so sheepishly are favourite subjects of knowledge allowed to oust questions of much greater import. What kind of lantern would be needed here, in order to find men capable of a complete surrender to genius, and of an intimate knowledge of its depths—men possessed of sufficient courage and strength to exorcise the demons that have forsaken our age? Viewed from the outside, such quarters certainly do appear to possess the whole pomp of culture; with their imposing apparatus they resemble great arsenals fitted with huge guns and other machinery of war; we see preparations in progress and the most strenuous activity, as though the heavens themselves were to be stormed, and truth were to be drawn out of the deepest of all wells; and yet, in war, the largest machines are the most unwieldy. Genuine culture therefore leaves such places as these religiously alone, for its best instincts warn it that in their midst it has nothing to hope for, and very much to fear. For the only kind of culture with which the inflamed eye and obtuse brain of the scholar working-classes concern themselves is of that Philistine order of which Strauss has announced the gospel. If we consider for a moment the fundamental causes underlying the sympathy which binds the learned working-classes to Culture-Philistinism, we shall discover the road leading to Strauss the Writer, who has been acknowledged classical, and tihence to our last and principal theme.

To begin with, that culture has contentment written in its every feature, and will allow of no important changes being introduced into the present state of German education. It is above all convinced of the originality of all German educational institutions, more particularly the public schools and universities; it does not cease recommending these to foreigners, and never doubts that if the Germans have become the most cultivated and discriminating people on earth, it is owing to such institutions. Culture-Philistinism believes in itself, consequently it also believes in the methods and means at its disposal. Secondly, however, it leaves the highest judgment concerning all questions of taste and culture to the scholar, and even regards itself as the ever-increasing compendium of scholarly opinions regarding art, literature, and philosophy. Its first care is to urge the scholar to express his opinions; these it proceeds to mix, dilute, and systematise, and then it administers them to the German people in the form of a bottle of medicine. What conies to life outside this circle is either not heard or attended at all, or if heard, is heeded half-heartedly; until, at last, a voice (it does not matter whose, provided it belong to some one who is strictly typical of the scholar tribe) is heard to issue from the temple in which traditional infallibility of taste is said to reside; and from that time forward public opinion has one conviction more, which it echoes and re-echoes hundreds and hundreds of times. As a matter of fact, though, the aesthetic infallibility of any utterance emanating from the temple is the more doubtful, seeing that the lack of taste, thought, and artistic feeling in any scholar can be taken for granted, unless it has previously been proved that, in his particular case, the reverse is true. And only a few can prove this. For how many who have had a share in the breathless and unending scurry of modern science have preserved that quiet and courageous gaze of the struggling man of culture—if they ever possessed it—that gaze which condemns even the scurry we speak of as a barbarous state of affairs? That is why these few are forced to live in an almost perpetual contradiction. What could they do against the uniform belief of the thousands who have enlisted public opinion in their cause, and who mutually defend each other in this belief? What purpose can it serve when one individual openly declares war against Strauss, seeing that a crowd have decided in his favour, and that the masses led by this crowd have learned to ask six consecutive times for the Master's Philistine sleeping-mixture?

If, without further ado, we here assumed that the Straussian confession-book had triumphed over public opinion and had been acclaimed and welcomed as conqueror, its author might call our attention to the fact that the multitudinous criticisms of his work in the various public organs are not of an altogether unanimous or even favourable character, and that he therefore felt it incumbent upon him to defend himself against some of the more malicious, impudent, and provoking of these newspaper pugilists by means of a postscript. How can there be a public opinion concerning my book, he cries to us, if every journalist is to regard me as an outlaw, and to mishandle me as much as he likes? This contradiction is easily explained, as soon as one considers the two aspects of the Straussian book—the theological and the literary, and it is only the latter that has anything to do with German culture. Thanks to its theological colouring, it stands beyond the pale of our German culture, and provokes the animosity of the various theological groups—yea, even of every individual German, in so far as he is a theological sectarian from birth, and only invents his own peculiar private belief in order to be able to dissent from every other form of belief. But when the question arises of talking about Strauss THE WRITER, pray listen to what the theological sectarians have to say about him. As soon as his literary side comes under notice, all theological objections immediately subside, and the dictum comes plain and clear, as if from the lips of one congregation: *In spite of it all, he is still a classical writer!*

Everybody—even the most bigoted, orthodox Churchman—pays the writer the most gratifying compliments, while there is always a word or two thrown in as a tribute to his almost Lessingesque language, his delicacy of touch, or the beauty and accuracy of his aesthetic views. As a book, therefore, the Straussian performance appears to meet all the demands of an ideal example of its kind. The theological opponents, despite the fact that their voices were the loudest of all, nevertheless constitute but an infinitesimal portion of the great public; and even with regard to them, Strauss still maintains that he is right when he says: "Compared with my thousands of readers, a few dozen public cavillers form but an insignificant minority, and they can hardly prove that they are their faithful interpreters. It was obviously in the nature of things that opposition should be clamorous and assent tacit." Thus, apart from the angry bitterness which Strauss's profession of faith may have provoked here and there, even the most fanatical of his opponents, to whom his voice seems to rise out of an abyss, like the voice of a beast, are agreed as to his merits as a writer; and that is why the treatment which Strauss has received at the hands of the literary lackeys of the theological groups proves nothing against our contention that Culture-Philistinism celebrated its triumph in this book. It must be admitted that the average educated Philistine is a degree less honest than Strauss, or is at least more reserved in his public utterances. But this fact only tends to increase his admiration for honesty in another. At home, or in the company of his equals, he may applaud with wild enthusiasm, but takes care not to put on paper how entirely Strauss's words are in harmony with his own innermost feelings. For, as we have already maintained, our Culture-Philistine is somewhat of a coward, even in his strongest sympathies; hence Strauss, who can boast of a trifle more courage than he, becomes his leader, notwithstanding the fact that even Straussian pluck has its very definite limits. If he overstepped these limits, as Schopenhauer does in almost every sentence, he would then forfeit his position at the head of the Philistines, and everybody would flee from him as precipitately as they are now following in his wake. He who would regard this artful if not sagacious moderation and this mediocre valour as an Aristotelian virtue, would certainly be wrong; for the valour in question is not the golden mean between two faults, but between a virtue and a fault— and in this mean, between virtue and fault, all Philistine qualities are to be found.

IX.

"In spite of it all, he is still a classical writer." Well, let us see! Perhaps we may now be allowed to discuss Strauss the stylist and master of language; but in the first place let us inquire whether, as a literary man, he is equal to the task of building his house, and whether he really understands the architecture of a book. From this inquiry we shall be able to conclude whether he is a respectable, thoughtful, and experienced author; and even should we be forced to answer "No" to these questions, he may still, as a last shift, take refuge in his fame as a classical prose-writer. This last-mentioned talent alone, it is true, would not suffice to class him with the classical authors, but at most with the classical improvisers and virtuosos of style, who, however, in regard to power of expression and the whole planning and framing of the work, reveal the awkward hand and the embarrassed eye of the bungler. We therefore put the question, whether Strauss really possesses the artistic strength necessary for the purpose of presenting us with a thing that is a whole, *totum ponere?*

As a rule, it ought to be possible to tell from the first rough sketch of a work whether the author conceived the thing as a whole, and whether, in view of this original conception, he has discovered the correct way of proceeding with his task and of fixing its proportions. Should this most important Part of the problem be solved, and should the framework of the building have been given its most favourable proportions, even then there remains enough to be done: how many smaller faults have to be corrected, how many gaps require filling in! Here and there a temporary partition or floor was found to answer the requirements; everywhere dust and fragments litter the ground, and no matter where we look, we see the signs of work done and work still to be done. The house, as a whole, is still uninhabitable and gloomy, its walls are bare, and the wind blows in through the open windows. Now, whether this remaining, necessary, and very irksome work has been satisfactorily accomplished by Strauss does not concern us at present; our question is, whether the building itself has been conceived as a whole, and whether its proportions are good? The reverse of this, of course, would be a compilation of fragments—a method generally adopted by scholars. They rely upon it that these fragments are related among themselves, and thus confound the logical and the artistic relation between them. Now, the relation between the four questions which provide the chapter-headings of Strauss's book cannot be called a logical one. Are we still Christians? Have we still a religion? What is our conception of the universe? What is our rule of life? And it is by no means contended that the relation is illogical simply because the third question has nothing to do with the second, nor the fourth with the third, nor all three with the first. The natural scientist who puts the third question, for instance, shows his unsullied love of truth by the simple fact that he tacitly passes over the second. And with regard to the subject of the fourth chapter—marriage, republicanism, and capital punishment—Strauss himself seems to have been aware that they could only have been muddled and obscured by being associated with the Darwinian theory expounded in the third chapter; for he carefully avoids all reference to this theory when discussing them. But the question, "Are we still Christians?" destroys the freedom of the philosophical standpoint at one stroke, by lending it an unpleasant theological colouring. Moreover, in this matter, he quite forgot that the majority of men to-day are not Christians at all, but Buddhists. Why should one, without further ceremony, immediately think of Christianity at the sound of the words "old faith"? Is this a sign that Strauss has never ceased to be a Christian theologian, and that he has therefore never learned to be a philosopher? For we find still greater cause for surprise in the fact that he quite fails to distinguish between belief and knowledge, and continually mentions his "new belief" and the still newer science in one breath. Or is "new belief" merely an ironical concession to ordinary parlance? This almost seems to be the case; for here and there he actually allows "new belief" and "newer science" to be interchangeable terms, as for instance on page II, where he asks on which side, whether on that of the ancient orthodoxy or of modern science, "exist more of the obscurities and insufficiencies unavoidable in human speculation."

Moreover, according to the scheme laid down in the Introduction, his desire is to disclose those proofs upon which the modern view of life is based; but he derives all these proofs from science, and in this respect assumes far more the attitude of a scientist than of a believer.

At bottom, therefore, the religion is not a new belief, but, being of a piece with modern science, it has nothing to do with religion at all. If Strauss, however, persists in his claims to be religious, the grounds for these claims must be beyond the pale of recent science. Only the smallest portion of the Straussian book—that is to say, but a few isolated pages—refer to what Strauss in all justice might call a belief, namely, that feeling for the "All" for which he demands the piety that the old believer demanded for his God. On the pages in question, however, he cannot claim to be altogether scientific; but if only he could lay claim to being a little stronger, more natural, more outspoken, more pious, we should be content. Indeed, what perhaps strikes us most forcibly about him is the multitude of artificial procedures of which he avails himself before he ultimately gets the feeling that he still possesses a belief and a religion; he reaches it by means of stings and blows, as we have already seen. How indigently and feebly this emergency-belief presents itself to us! We shiver at the sight of it.

Although Strauss, in the plan laid down in his Introduction, promises to compare the two faiths, the old and the new, and to show that the latter will answer the same purpose as the former, even *he* begins to feel, in the end, that he has promised too much. For the question whether the new belief answers the same purpose as the old, or is better or worse, is disposed of incidentally, so to speak, and with uncomfortable haste, in two or three pages (p. 436 et seq.-), and is actually bolstered up by the following subterfuge: "He who cannot help himself in this matter is beyond help, is not yet ripe for our standpoint" (p. 436). How differently, and with what intensity of conviction, did the ancient Stoic believe in the All and the rationality of the All! And, viewed in this light, how does Strauss's claim to originality appear? But, as we have already observed, it would be a matter of indifference to us whether it were new, old, original, or imitated, so that it were only more powerful, more healthy, and more natural. Even Strauss himself leaves this double-distilled emergency-belief to take care of itself as often as he can do so, in order to protect himself and us from danger, and to present his recently acquired biological knowledge to his "We" with a clear conscience. The more embarrassed he may happen to be when he speaks of faith, the rounder and fuller his mouth becomes when he quotes the greatest benefactor to modern men-Darwin. Then he not only exacts belief for the new Messiah, but also for himself—the new apostle. For instance, while discussing one of the most intricate questions in natural history, he declares with true ancient pride: "I shall be told that I am here speaking of things about which I understand nothing. Very well; but others will come who will understand them, and who will also have understood me" (p. 241).

According to this, it would almost seem as though the famous "We" were not only in duty bound to believe in the "All," but also in the naturalist Strauss; in this case we can only hope that in order to acquire the feeling for this last belief, other processes are requisite than the painful and cruel ones demanded by the first belief. Or is it perhaps sufficient in this case that the subject of belief himself be tormented and stabbed with the view of bringing the believers to that "religious reaction" which is the distinguishing sign of the "new faith." What merit should we then discover in the piety of those whom Strauss calls "We"?

Otherwise, it is almost to be feared that modern men will pass on in pursuit of their business without troubling themselves overmuch concerning the new furniture of faith offered them by the apostle: just as they have done heretofore, without the doctrine of the rationality of the All. The whole of modern biological and historical research has nothing to do with the Straussian belief in the All, and the fact that the modern Philistine does not require the belief is proved by the description of his life given by Strauss in the chapter,"What is our Rule of Life?" He is therefore quite right in doubting whether the coach to which his esteemed readers have been obliged to trust themselves "with him, fulfils every requirement." It certainly does not; for the modern man makes more rapid progress when he does not take his place in the Straussian coach, or rather, he got ahead much more quickly long before the Straussian coach ever existed. Now, if it be true that the famous "minority" which is "not to be overlooked," and of which, and in whose name, Strauss speaks, "attaches great importance to consistency," it must be just as dissatisfied with Strauss the Coachbuilder as we are with Strauss the Logician.

Let us, however, drop the question of the logician. Perhaps, from the artistic point of view, the book really is an example of a. well-conceived plan, and does, after all, answer to the requirements of the laws of beauty, despite the fact that it fails to meet with the demands of a well-conducted argument. And now, having shown that he is neither a scientist nor a strictly correct and systematic scholar, for the first time we approach the question: Is Strauss a capable writer? Perhaps the task he set himself was not so much to scare people away from the old faith as to captivate them by a picturesque and graceful description of what life would be with the new. If he regarded scholars and educated men as his most probable audience, experience ought certainly to have told him that whereas one can shoot such men down with the heavy guns of scientific proof, but cannot make them surrender, they may be got to capitulate all the more quickly before "lightly equipped" measures of seduction. "Lightly equipped," and "intentionally so," thus Strauss himself speaks of his own book. Nor do his public eulogisers refrain from using the same expression in reference to the work, as the following passage, quoted from one of the least remarkable among them, and in which the same expression is merely paraphrased, will go to prove:—

"The discourse flows on with delightful harmony: wherever it directs its criticism against old ideas it wields the art of demonstration, almost playfully; and it is with some spirit that it prepares the new ideas it brings so enticingly, and presents them to the simple as well as to the fastidious taste. The arrangement of such diverse and conflicting material is well thought out for every portion of it required to be touched upon, without being made too prominent; at times the transitions leading from one subject to another are artistically managed, and one hardly knows what to admire most—the skill with which unpleasant questions are shelved, or the discretion with which they are hushed up."

The spirit of such eulogies, as the above clearly shows, is not quite so subtle in regard to judging of what an author is able to do as in regard to what he wishes. What Strauss wishes, however, is best revealed by his own emphatic and not quite harmless commendation of Voltaire's charms, in whose service he might have learned precisely those "lightly equipped" arts of which his admirer speaks—granting, of course, that virtue may be acquired and a pedagogue can ever be a dancer.

Who could help having a suspicion or two, when reading the following passage, for instance, in which Strauss says of Voltaire, "As a philosopher [he] is certainly not original, but in the main a mere exponent of English investigations: in this respect, however, he shows himself to be completely master of his subject, which he presents with incomparable skill, in all possible lights and from all possible sides, and is able withal to meet the demands of thoroughness, without, however, being over-severe in his method"? Now, all the negative traits mentioned in this passage might be applied to Strauss. No one would contend, I suppose, that Strauss is original, or that he is over-severe in his method; but the question is whether we can regard him as "master of his subject," and grant him "incomparable skill"? The confession to the effect that the treatise was intentionally "lightly equipped" leads us to think that it at least aimed at incomparable skill.

It was not the dream of our architect to build a temple, nor yet a house, but a sort of summer-pavilion, surrounded by everything that the art of gardening can provide. Yea, it even seems as if that mysterious feeling for the All were only calculated to produce an aesthetic effect, to be, so to speak, a view of an irrational element, such as the sea, looked at from the most charming and rational of terraces. The walk through the first chapters— that is to say, through the theological catacombs with all their gloominess and their involved and baroque embellishments—was also no more than an aesthetic expedient in order to throw into greater relief the purity, clearness, and common sense of the chapter "What is our Conception of the Universe?" For, immediately after that walk in the gloaming and that peep into the wilderness of Irrationalism, we step into a hall with a skylight to it. Soberly and limpidly it welcomes us: its mural decorations consist of astronomical charts and mathematical figures; it is filled with scientific apparatus, and its cupboards contain skeletons, stuffed apes, and anatomical specimens. But now, really rejoicing for the first time, we direct our steps into the innermost chamber of bliss belonging to our pavilion-dwellers; there we find them with their wives, children, and newspapers, occupied in the commonplace discussion of politics; we listen for a moment to their conversation on marriage, universal suffrage, capital punishment, and workmen's strikes, and we can scarcely believe it to be possible that the rosary of public opinions can be told off so quickly. At length an attempt is made to convince us of the classical taste of the inmates. A moment's halt in the library, and the music-room suffices to show us what we had expected all along, namely, that the best books lay on the shelves, and that the most famous musical compositions were in the music-cabinets. Some one actually played something to us, and even if it were Haydn's music, Haydn could not be blamed because it sounded like Riehl's music for the home. Meanwhile the host had found occasion to announce to us his complete agreement with Lessing and Goethe, although with the latter only up to the second part of Faust. At last our pavilion-owner began to praise himself, and assured us that he who could not be happy under his roof was beyond help and could not be ripe for his standpoint, whereupon he offered us his coach, but with the polite reservation that he could not assert that it would fulfil every requirement, and that, owing to the stones on his road having been newly laid down, we were not to mind if we were very much jolted. Our Epicurean garden-god then took leave of us with the incomparable skill which he praised in Voltaire.

Who could now persist in doubting the existence of this incomparable skill? The complete master of his subject is revealed; the lightly equipped artist-gardener is exposed, and still we hear the voice of the classical author saying, "As a writer I shall for once cease to be a Philistine: I will not be one; I refuse to be one! But a Voltaire—the German Voltaire—or at least the French Lessing."

With this we have betrayed a secret. Our Master does not always know which he prefers to be—Voltaire or Lessing; but on no account will he be a Philistine. At a pinch he would not object to being both Lessing and

Voltaire—that the word might be fulfilled that is written, "He had no character, but when he wished to appear as if he had, he assumed one."

X.

If we have understood Strauss the Confessor correctly, he must be a genuine Philistine, with a narrow, parched soul and scholarly and common-place needs; albeit no one would be more indignant at the title than David Strauss the Writer. He would be quite happy to be regarded as mischievous, bold, malicious, daring; but his ideal of bliss would consist in finding himself compared with either Lessing or Voltaire—because these men were undoubtedly anything but Philistines. In striving after this state of bliss, he often seems to waver between two alternatives—either to mimic the brave and dialectical petulance of Lessing, or to affect the manner of the faun-like and free-spirited man of antiquity that Voltaire was. When taking up his pen to write, he seems to be continually posing for his portrait; and whereas at times his features are drawn to look like Lessing's, anon they are made to assume the Voltairean mould. While reading his praise of Voltaire's manner, we almost seem to see him abjuring the consciences of his contemporaries for not having learned long ago what the modern Voltaire had to offer them. "Even his excellences are wonderfully uniform," he says: "simple naturalness, transparent clearness, vivacious mobility, seductive charm. Warmth and emphasis are also not wanting where they are needed, and Voltaire's innermost nature always revolted against stiltedness and affectation; while, on the other hand, if at times wantonness or passion descend to an unpleasantly low level, the fault does not rest so much with the stylist as with the man." According to this, Strauss seems only too well aware of the importance of *simplicity in style*; it is ever the sign of genius, which alone has the privilege to express itself naturally and guilelessly. When, therefore, an author selects a simple mode of expression, this is no sign whatever of vulgar ambition; for although many are aware of what such an author would fain be taken for, they are yet kind enough to take him precisely for that. The genial writer, however, not only reveals his true nature in the plain and unmistakable form of his utterance, but his super-abundant strength actually dallies with the material he treats, even when it is dangerous and difficult. Nobody treads stiffly along unknown paths, especially when these are broken throughout their course by thousands of crevices and furrows; but the genius speeds nimbly over them, and, leaping with grace and daring, scorns the wistful and timorous step of caution.

Even Strauss knows that the problems he prances over are dreadfully serious, and have ever been regarded as such by the philosophers who have grappled with them; yet he calls his book *lightly equipped!* But of this dreadfulness and of the usual dark nature of our meditations when considering such questions as the worth of existence and the duties of man, we entirely cease to be conscious when the genial Master plays his antics before us, "lightly equipped, and intentionally so." Yes, even more lightly equipped than his Rousseau, of whom he tells us it was said that he stripped himself below and adorned himself on top, whereas Goethe did precisely the reverse. Perfectly guileless geniuses do not, it appears, adorn themselves at all; possibly the words "lightly equipped" may simply be a euphemism for "naked." The few who happen to have seen the Goddess of Truth declare that she is naked, and perhaps, in the minds of those who have never seen her, but who implicitly believe those few, nakedness or light equipment is actually a proof, or at least a feature, of truthi Even this vulgar superstition turns to the advantage of the author's ambition. Some one sees something naked, and he exclaims: "What if this were the truth!" Whereupon he grows more solemn than is his wont. By this means, however, the author scores a tremendous advantage; for he compels his reader to approach him with greater solemnity than another and perhaps more heavily equipped writer. This is unquestionably the best way to become a classical author; hence Strauss himself is able to tell us: "I even enjoy the unsought honour of being, in the opinion of many, a classical writer of prose. "He has therefore achieved his aim. Strauss the Genius goes gadding about the streets in the garb of lightly equipped goddesses as a classic, while Strauss the Philistine, to use an original expression of this genius's, must, at all costs, be "declared to be on the decline," or "irrevocably dismissed."

But, alas! in spite of all declarations of decline and dismissal, the Philistine still returns, and all too frequently. Those features, contorted to resemble Lessing and Voltaire, must relax from time to time to resume their old and original shape. The mask of genius falls from them too often, and the Master's expression is never more sour and his movements never stiffer than when he has just attempted to take the leap, or to glance with the fiery eye, of a genius. Precisely owing to the fact that he is too lightly equipped for our zone, he runs the risk of catching cold more often and more severely than another. It may seem a terrible hardship to him that every one should notice this; but if he wishes to be cured, the following diagnosis of his case ought to be publicly presented to him:— Once upon a time there lived a Strauss, a brave, severe, and stoutly equipped scholar, with whom we sympathised as wholly as with all those in Germany who seek to serve truth with earnestness and energy, and to rule within the limits of their powers. He, however, who is now publicly famous as David Strauss, is another person. The theologians may be to blame for this metamorphosis; but, at any rate, his present toying with the mask of genius inspires us with as much hatred and scorn as his former earnestness commanded respect and sympathy. When, for instance, he tells us, "it would also argue ingratitude towards *my genius* if I were not to rejoice that to the faculty of an incisive, analytical criticism was added the innocent pleasure in artistic production," it may astonish him to hear that, in spite of this self-praise, there are still men who maintain exactly the reverse, and who say, not only that he has never possessed the gift of artistic production, but that the "innocent" pleasure he mentions is of all things the least innocent, seeing that it succeeded in gradually undermining and ultimately destroying a nature as strongly and deeply scholarly and critical as Strauss's—in fact, *the real Straussian Genius*. In a moment of unlimited frankness, Strauss himself indeed adds: "Merck was always in my thoughts, calling out, 'Don't produce such child's play again; others can do that too!'" That was the voice of the real Straussian genius, which also asked him what the worth of his newest, innocent, and lightly equipped modern Philistine's testament was. Others can do that too! And many could do it better. And even they who could have done it best, i.e. those thinkers who are more widely endowed than Strauss, could still only have made nonsense of it.

I take it that you are now beginning to understand the value I set on Strauss the Writer. You are beginning to realise that I regard him as a mummer who would parade as an artless genius and classical writer. When Lichtenberg said, "A simple manner of writing is to be recommended, if only in view of the fact that no honest man trims and twists his expressions," he was very far from wishing to imply that a simple style is a proof of literary integrity. I, for my part, only wish that Strauss the Writer had been more upright, for then he would have written more becomingly and have been less famous. Or, if he would be a mummer at all costs, how much more would he not have pleased me if he had been a better mummer—one more able to ape the guileless genius and classical author! For it yet remains to be said that Strauss was not only an inferior actor but a very worthless stylist as well.

XI.

Of course, the blame attaching to Strauss for being a bad writer is greatly mitigated by the fact that it is extremely difficult in Germany to become even a passable or moderately good writer, and that it is more the exception than not, to be a really good one. In this respect the natural soil is wanting, as are also artistic values and the proper method of treating and cultivating oratory. This latter accomplishment, as the various branches of it, i.e. drawing-room, ecclesiastical and Parliamentary parlance, show, has not yet reached the level of a national style; indeed, it has not yet shown even a tendency to attain to a style at all, and all forms of language in Germany do not yet seem to have passed a certain experimental stage. In view of these facts, the writer of to-day, to some extent, lacks an authoritative standard, and he is in some measure excused if, in the matter of language, he attempts to go ahead of his own accord. As to the probable result which the present dilapidated condition of the German language will bring about, Schopenhauer, perhaps, has spoken most forcibly. "If the existing state of affairs continues," he says, "in the year 1900 German classics will cease to be understood, for the simple reason that no other language will be known, save the trumpery jargon of the noble present, the chief characteristic of which is impotence." And, in truth, if one turn to the latest periodicals, one will find German philologists and grammarians already giving expression to the view that our classics can no longer serve us as examples of style, owing to the fact that they constantly use words, modes of speech, and syntactic arrangements which are fast dropping out of currency. Hence the need of collecting specimens of the finest prose that has been produced by our best modern writers, and of offering them as examples to be followed, after the style of Sander's pocket dictionary of bad language. In this book, that repulsive monster of style Gutzkow appears as a classic, and, according to its injunctions, we seem to be called upon to accustom ourselves to quite a new and wondrous crowd of classical authors, among which the first, or one of the first, is David Strauss: he whom we cannot describe more aptly than we have already—that is to say, as a worthless stylist. Now, the notion which the Culture-Philistine has of a classic and standard author speaks eloquently for his pseudo-culture—he who only shows his strength by opposing a really artistic and severe style, and who, thanks to the persistence of his opposition, finally arrives at a certain uniformity of expression, which again almost appears to possess unity of genuine style. In view, therefore, of the right which is granted to every one to experiment with the language, how is it possible at all for individual authors to discover a generally agreeable tone? What is so generally interesting in them? In the first place, a negative quality—the total lack of offensiveness: but *every really productive thing is offensive.* The greater part of a German's daily reading matter is undoubtedly sought either in the pages of newspapers, periodicals, or reviews. The language of these journals gradually stamps itself on his brain, by means of its steady drip, drip, drip of similar phrases and similar words. And, since he generally devotes to reading those hours of the day during which his exhausted brain is in any case not inclined to offer resistance, his ear for his native tongue so slowly but surely accustoms itself to this everyday German that it ultimately cannot endure its absence without pain. But the manufacturers of these newspapers are, by virtue of their trade, most thoroughly inured to the effluvia of this journalistic jargon; they have literally lost all taste, and their palate is rather gratified than not by the most corrupt and arbitrary innovations. Hence the tutti unisono with which, despite the general lethargy and sickliness, every fresh solecism is greeted; it is with such impudent corruptions of the language that her hirelings are avenged against her for the incredible boredom she imposes ever more and more upon them. I remember having read "an appeal to the German nation," by Berthold Auerbach, in which every sentence was un-German, distorted and false, and which, as a whole, resembled a soulless mosaic of words cemented together with international syntax. As to the disgracefully slipshod German with which Edward

Devrient solemnised the death of Mendelssohn, I do not even wish to do more than refer to it. A grammatical error—and this is the most extraordinary feature of the case—does not therefore seem an offence in any sense to our Philistine, but a most delightful restorative in the barren wilderness of everyday German. He still, however, considers all *really* productive things to be offensive. The wholly bombastic, distorted, and threadbare syntax of the modern standard author—yea, even his ludicrous neologisms—are not only tolerated, but placed to his credit as the spicy element in his works. But woe to the stylist with character, who seeks as earnestly and perseveringly to avoid the trite phrases of everyday parlance, as the "yester-night monster blooms of modern ink-flingers," as Schopenhauer says! When platitudes, hackneyed, feeble, and vulgar phrases are the rule, and the bad and the corrupt become refreshing exceptions, then all that is strong, distinguished, and beautiful perforce acquires an evil odour. From which it follows that, in Germany, the well-known experience which befell the normally built traveller in the land of hunchbacks is constantly being repeated. It will be remembered that he was so shamefully insulted there, owing to his quaint figure and lack of dorsal convexity, that a priest at last had to harangue the people on his behalf as follows: "My brethren, rather pity this poor stranger, and present thank-offerings unto the gods, that ye are blessed with such attractive gibbosities."

If any one attempted to compose a positive grammar out of the international German style of to-day, and wished to trace the unwritten and unspoken laws followed by every one, he would get the most extraordinary notions of style and rhetoric. He would meet with laws which are probably nothing more than reminiscences of bygone schooldays, vestiges of impositions for Latin prose, and results perhaps of choice readings from French novelists, over whose incredible crudeness every decently educated Frenchman would have the right to laugh. But no conscientious native of Germany seems to have given a thought to these extraordinary notions under the yoke of which almost every German lives and writes.

As an example of what I say, we may find an injunction to the effect that a metaphor or a simile must be introduced from time to time, and that it must be new; but, since to the mind of the shallow-pated writer newness and modernity are identical, he proceeds forthwith to rack his brain for metaphors in the technical vocabularies of the railway, the telegraph, the steamship, and the Stock Exchange, and is proudly convinced that such metaphors must be new because they are modern. In Strauss's confession-book we find liberal tribute paid to modern metaphor. He treats us to a simile, covering a page and a half, drawn from modern road-improvement work; a few pages farther back he likens the world to a machine, with its wheels, stampers, hammers, and "soothing oil" (p. 432); "A repast that begins with champagne" (p. 384); "Kant is a cold-water cure" (p. 309); "The Swiss constitution is to that of England as a watermill is to a steam-engine, as a waltz-tune or a song to a fugue or symphony" (p. 301); "In every appeal, the sequence of procedure must be observed. Now the mean tribunal between the individual and humanity is the nation" (p. 165); "If we would know whether there be still any life in an organism which appears dead to us, we are wont to test it by a powerful, even painful stimulus, as for example a stab" (p. 161); "The religious domain in the human soul resembles the domain of the Red Indian in America" (p. 160); "Virtuosos in piety, in convents"(p. 107); "And place the sum-total of the foregoing in round numbers under the account" (p. 205); "Darwin's theory resembles a railway track that is just marked out... where the flags are fluttering joyfully in the breeze." In this really highly modern way, Strauss has met the Philistine injunction to the effect that a new simile must be introduced from time to time.

Another rhetorical rule is also very widespread, namely, that didactic passages should be composed in long periods, and should be drawn out into lengthy abstractions, while all persuasive passages should consist of short sentences followed by striking contrasts. On page 154 in Strauss's book we find a standard example of the didactic and scholarly style—a passage blown out after the genuine Schleiermacher manner, and made to stumble along at a true tortoise pace: "The reason why, in the earlier stages of religion, there appear many instead of this single Whereon, a plurality of gods instead of the one, is explained in this deduction of religion, from the fact that the various forces of nature, or relations of life, which inspire man with the sentiment of unqualified dependence, still act upon him in the commencement with the full force of their distinctive characteristics; that he has not as yet become conscious how, in regard to his unmitigated dependence upon them, there is no distinction between them, and that therefore the Whereon of this dependence, or the Being to which it conducts in the last instance, can only be one."

On pages 7 and 8 we find an example of the other kind of style, that of the short sentences containing that affected liveliness which so excited certain readers that they cannot mention Strauss any more without coupling his name with Lessing's. "I am well aware that what I propose to delineate in the following pages is known to multitudes as well as to myself, to some even much better. A few have already spoken out on the subject. Am I therefore to keep silence? I think not. For do we not all supply each other's deficiencies? If another is better informed as regards some things, I may perhaps be so as regards others; while yet others are known and viewed by me in a different light. Out with it, then! let my colours be displayed that it may be seen whether they are genuine or not.'"

It is true that Strauss's style generally maintains a happy medium between this sort of merry quick-march and the other funereal and indolent pace; but between two vices one does not invariably find a virtue; more often rather only weakness, helpless paralysis, and impotence. As a matter of fact, I was very disappointed when I glanced through Strauss's book in search of fine and witty passages; for, not having found anything praiseworthy in the Confessor, I had actually set out with the express purpose of meeting here and there with at least some opportunities of praising Strauss the Writer. I sought and sought, but my purpose remained unfulfilled. Meanwhile, however, another duty seemed to press itself strongly on my mind—that of enumerating the solecisms, the strained metaphors, the obscure abbreviations, the instances of bad taste, and the distortions which I encountered; and these were of such a nature that I dare do no more than select a few examples of them from among a collection which is too bulky to be given in full. By means of these examples I may succeed in showing what it is that inspires, in the hearts of modern Germans, such faith in this great and seductive stylist Strauss: I refer to his eccentricities of expression, which, in the barren waste and dryness of his whole book, jump out at one, not perhaps as pleasant but as painfully stimulating, surprises. When perusing such passages, we are at least assured, to use a Straussian metaphor, that we are not quite dead, but still respond to the test of a stab. For the rest of the book is entirely lacking in offensiveness —that quality which alone, as we have seen, is productive, and which our classical author has himself reckoned among the positive virtues. When the educated masses meet with exaggerated dulness and dryness, when they are in the presence of really vapid commonplaces, they now seem to believe that such things are the signs of health; and in this respect the words of the author of the dialogus de oratoribus are very much to the point: "illam ipsam quam jactant sanitatem non firmitate sed jejunio consequuntur." That is why they so unanimously hate every firmitas, because it bears testimony to a kind of health quite different from theirs; hence their one wish to throw suspicion upon all austerity and terseness, upon all fiery and energetic movement, and upon every full and delicate play of muscles. They have conspired to twist nature and the names of things completely round, and for the future to speak of health only there where we see weakness, and to speak of illness and excitability where for our part we see genuine vigour. From which it follows that David Strauss is to them a classical author.

If only this dulness were of a severely logical order! but simplicity and austerity in thought are precisely what these weaklings have lost, and in their hands even our language has become illogically tangled. As a proof of this, let any one try to translate Strauss's style into Latin: in the case of Kant, be it remembered, this is possible, while with Schopenhauer it even becomes an agreeable exercise. The reason why this test fails with Strauss's German is not owing to the fact that it is more Teutonic than theirs, but because his is distorted and illogical, whereas theirs is lofty and simple. Moreover, he who knows how the ancients exerted themselves in order to learn to write and speak correctly, and how the moderns omit to do so, must feel, as Schopenhauer says, a positive relief when he can turn from a German book like the one under our notice, to dive into those other works, those ancient works which seem to him still to be written in a new language. "For in these books," says Schopenhauer, "I find a regular and fixed language which, throughout, faithfully follows the laws of grammar and orthography, so that I can give up my thoughts completely to their matter; whereas in German I am constantly being disturbed by the author's impudence and his continual attempts to establish his own orthographical freaks and absurd ideas— the swaggering foolery of which disgusts me. It is really a painful sight to see a fine old language, possessed of classical literature, being botched by asses and ignoramuses!"

Thus Schopenhauer's holy anger cries out to us, and you cannot say that you have not been warned. He who turns a deaf ear to such warnings, and who absolutely refuses to relinquish his faith in Strauss the classical author, can only be given this last word of advice—to imitate his hero. In any case, try it at your own risk; but you will repent it, not only in your style but in your head, that it may be fulfilled which was spoken by the Indian prophet, saying, "He who gnaweth a cow's horn gnaweth in vain and shorteneth his life; for he grindeth away his teeth, yet his belly is empty."

XII.

By way of concluding, we shall proceed to give our classical prose-writer the promised examples of his style which we have collected. Schopenhauer would probably have classed the whole lot as "new documents serving to swell the trumpery jargon of the present day"; for David Strauss may be comforted to hear (if what follows can be regarded as a comfort at all) that everybody now writes as he does; some, of course, worse, and that among the blind the one-eyed is king. Indeed, we allow him too much when we grant him one eye; but we do this willingly, because Strauss does not write so badly as the most infamous of all corrupters of German—the Hegelians and their crippled offspring. Strauss at least wishes to extricate himself from the mire, and he is already partly out of it; still, he is very far from being on dry land, and he still shows signs of having stammered Hegel's prose in youth. In those days, possibly, something was sprained in him, some muscle must have been overstrained. His ear, perhaps, like that of a boy brought up amid the beating of drums, grew dull, and became incapable of detecting those artistically subtle and yet mighty laws of sound, under the guidance of which every writer is content to remain who has been strictly trained in the study of good models. But in this way, as a stylist, he has lost his most valuable possessions, and stands condemned to remain reclining, his life long, on the dangerous and barren shifting sand of newspaper style—that is, if he do not wish to fall back into the Hegelian mire. Nevertheless, he has succeeded in making himself famous for a couple of hours in our time, and perhaps in another couple of hours people will remember that he was once famous; then, however, night will come, and with her oblivion; and already at this moment, while we are entering his sins against style in the black book, the sable mantle of twilight is falling upon his fame. For he who has sinned against the German language has desecrated the mystery of all our Germanity. Throughout all the confusion and the changes of races and of customs, the German language alone, as though possessed of some supernatural charm, has saved herself; and with her own salvation she has wrought that of the spirit of Germany. She alone holds the warrant for this spirit in future ages, provided she be not destroyed at the sacrilegious hands of the modern world. "But *Di meliora!* Avaunt, ye pachyderms, avaunt! This is the German language, by means of which men express themselves, and in which great poets have sung and great thinkers have written. Hands off!" *

[Footnote * : Translator's note.—Nietzsche here proceeds to quote those passages he has culled from *The Old and the New Faith* with which he undertakes to substantiate all he has said relative to Strauss's style; as, however, these passages, with his comments upon them, lose most of their point when rendered into English, it was thought best to omit them altogether.]

To put it in plain words, what we have seen have been feet of clay, and what appeared to be of the colour of healthy flesh was only applied paint. Of course, Culture-Philistinism in Germany will be very angry when it hears its one living God referred to as a series of painted idols. He, however, who dares to overthrow its idols will not shrink, despite all indignation, from telling it to its face that it has forgotten how to distinguish between the quick and the dead, the genuine and the counterfeit, the original and the imitation, between a God and a host of idols; that it has completely lost the healthy and manly instinct for what is real and right. It alone deserves to be destroyed; and already the manifestations of its power are sinking; already are its purple honours falling from it; but when the purple falls, its royal wearer soon follows.

Here I come to the end of my confession of faith. This is the confession of an individual; and what can such an one do against a whole world, even supposing his voice were heard everywhere! In order for the last time to use a precious Straussism, his judgment only possesses *"that amount of subjective truth which is compatible with a complete lack of objective demonstration"*—is not that so, my dear friends? Meanwhile, be of good cheer. For the time being let the matter rest at this "amount which is compatible with a complete lack"! For the time being! That is to say, for as long as that is held to be out of season which in reality is always in season, and is now more than ever pressing; I refer to...speaking the truth.*

[Footnote *: Translator's note.—All quotations from The Old Faith and the New which appear in the above translation have either been taken bodily out of Mathilde Blind's translation (Asher and Co., 1873), or are adaptations from that translation.]

RICHARD WAGNER IN BAYREUTH.

I.

FOR an event to be great, two things must be united—the lofty sentiment of those who accomplish it, and the lofty sentiment of those who witness it. No event is great in itself, even though it be the disappearance of whole constellations, the destruction of several nations, the establishment of vast empires, or the prosecution of wars at the cost of enormous forces: over things of this sort the breath of history blows as if they were flocks of wool. But it often happens, too, that a man of might strikes a blow which falls without effect upon a stubborn stone; a short, sharp report is heard, and all is over. History is able to record little or nothing of such abortive efforts. Hence the anxiety which every one must feel who, observing the approach of an event, wonders whether those about to witness it will be worthy of it. This reciprocity between an act and its reception is always taken into account when anything great or small is to be accomplished; and he who would give anything away must see to it that he find recipients who will do justice to the meaning of his gift. This is why even the work of a great man is not necessarily great when it is short, abortive, or fruitless; for at the moment when he performed it he must have failed to perceive that it was really necessary; he must have been careless in his aim, and he cannot have chosen and fixed upon the time with sufficient caution. Chance thus became his master; for there is a very intimate relation between greatness and the instinct which discerns the proper moment at which to act.

We therefore leave it to those who doubt Wagner's power of discerning the proper time for action, to be concerned and anxious as to whether what is now taking place in Bayreuth is really opportune and necessary. To us who are more confident, it is clear that he believes as strongly in the greatness of his feat as in the greatness of feeling in those who are to witness it. Be their number great or small, therefore, all those who inspire this faith in Wagner should feel extremely honoured; for that it was not inspired by everybody, or by the whole age, or even by the whole German people, as they are now constituted, he himself told us in his dedicatory address of the 22nd of May 1872, and not one amongst us could, with any show of conviction, assure him of the contrary. "I had only you to turn to," he said, "when I sought those who I thought would be in sympathy with my plans,— you who are the most personal friends of my own particular art, my work and activity: only you could I invite to help me in my work, that it might be presented pure and whole to those who manifest a genuine interest in my art, despite the fact that it has hitherto made its appeal to them only in a disfigured and adulterated form."

It is certain that in Bayreuth even the spectator is a spectacle worth seeing. If the spirit of some observant sage were to return, after the absence of a century, and were to compare the most remarkable movements in the present world of culture, he would find much to interest him there. Like one swimming in a lake, who encounters a current of warm water issuing from a hot spring, in Bayreuth he would certainly feel as though he had suddenly plunged into a more temperate element, and would tell himself that this must rise out of a distant and deeper source: the surrounding mass of water, which at all events is more common in origin, does not account for it. In this way, all those who assist at the Bayreuth festival will seem like men out of season; their raison-d'etre and the forces which would seem to account for them are elsewhere, and their home is not in the present age. I realise ever more clearly that the scholar, in so far as he is entirely the man of his own day, can only be accessible to all that Wagner does and thinks by means of parody,—and since everything is parodied nowadays, he will even get the event of Bayreuth reproduced for him, through the very un-magic lanterns of our facetious art-critics. And one ought to be thankful if they stop at parody; for by means of it a spirit of aloofness and animosity finds a vent which might otherwise hit upon a less desirable mode of expression. Now, the observant sage already mentioned could not remain blind to this unusual sharpness and tension of contrasts. They who hold by gradual development as a kind of moral law must be somewhat shocked at the sight of one who, in the course of a single lifetime, succeeds in producing something absolutely new. Being dawdlers themselves, and insisting upon slowness as a principle, they are very naturally vexed by one who strides rapidly ahead, and they wonder how on earth he does it. No omens, no periods of transition, and no concessions preceded the enterprise at Bayreuth; no one except Wagner knew either the goal or the long road that was to lead to it. In the realm of art it signifies, so to speak, the first circumnavigation of the world, and by this voyage not only was there discovered an apparently new art, but Art itself. In view of this, all modern arts, as arts of luxury which have degenerated through having been insulated, have become almost worthless. And the same applies to the nebulous and inconsistent reminiscences of a genuine art, which we as modern Europeans derive from the Greeks; let them rest in peace, unless they are now able to shine of their own accord in the light of a new interpretation. The last hour has come for a good many things; this new art is a clairvoyante that sees ruin approaching—not for art alone. Her warning voice must strike the whole of our prevailing civilisation with terror the instant the laughter which its parodies have provoked subsides. Let it laugh and enjoy itself for yet a while longer!

And as for us, the disciples of this revived art, we shall have time and inclination for thoughtfulness, deep thoughtfulness. All the talk and noise about art which has been made by civilisation hitherto must seem like shameless obtrusiveness; everything makes silence a duty with us—the quinquennial silence of the Pythagoreans. Which of us has not soiled his hands and heart in the disgusting idolatry of modern culture? Which of us can exist without the waters of purification? Who does not hear the voice which cries, "Be silent and cleansed"? Be silent and cleansed! Only the merit of being included among those who give ear to this voice will grant even us the *lofty look* necessary to view the event at Bayreuth; and only upon this look depends the *great future* of the event.

When on that dismal and cloudy day in May 1872, after the foundation stone had been laid on the height of Bayreuth, amid torrents of rain, and while Wagner was driving back to the town with a small party of us, he was exceptionally silent, and there was that indescribable look in his eyes as of one who has turned his gaze deeply inwards. The day happened to be the first of his sixtieth year, and his whole past now appeared as but a long preparation for this great moment. It is almost a recognised fact that in times of exceptional danger, or at all decisive and culminating points in their lives, men see the remotest and most recent events of their career with singular vividness, and in one rapid inward glance obtain a sort of panorama of a whole span of years in which every event is faithfully depicted. What, for instance, must Alexander the Great have seen in that instant when he caused Asia and Europe to be drunk out of the same goblet? But what went through Wagner's mind on that day—how he became what he is, and what he will be—we only can imagine who are nearest to him, and can follow him, up to a certain point, in his self-examination; but through his eyes alone is it possible for us to understand his grand work, and by the help of this understanding vouch for its fruitfulness.

II.

It were strange if what a man did best and most liked to do could not be traced in the general outline of his life, and in the case of those who are remarkably endowed there is all the more reason for supposing that their life will present not only the counterpart of their character, as in the case of every one else, but that it will present above all the counterpart of their intellect and their most individual tastes. The life of the epic poet will have a dash of the Epos in it—as from all accounts was the case with Goethe, whom the Germans very wrongly regarded only as a lyrist—and the life of the dramatist will probably be dramatic.

The dramatic element in Wagner's *development* cannot be ignored, from the time when his ruling passion became self-conscious and took possession of his whole being. From that time forward there is an end to all groping, straying, and sprouting of offshoots, and over his most tortuous deviations and excursions, over the often eccentric disposition of his plans, a single law and will are seen to rule, in which we have the explanation of his actions, however strange this explanation may sometimes appear. There was, however, an ante-dramatic period in Wagner's life—his childhood and youth— which it is impossible to approach without discovering innumerable problems. At this period there seems to be no promise yet of himself, and what one might now, in a retrospect, regard as a pledge for his future greatness, amounts to no more than a juxtaposition of traits which inspire more dismay than hope; a restless and excitable spirit, nervously eager to undertake a hundred things at the same time, passionately fond of almost morbidly exalted states of mind, and ready at any moment to veer completely round from calm and profound meditation to a state of violence and uproar. In his case there were no hereditary or family influences at work to constrain him to the sedulous study of one particular art. Painting, versifying, acting, and music were just as much within his reach as the learning and the career of a scholar; and the superficial inquirer into this stage of his life might even conclude that he was born to be a dilettante. The small world within the bounds of which he grew up was not of the kind we should choose to be the home of an artist. He ran the constant risk of becoming infected by that dangerously dissipated attitude of mind in which a person will taste of everything, as also by that condition of slackness resulting from the fragmentary knowledge of all things, which is so characteristic of University towns. His feelings were easily roused and but indifferently satisfied; wherever the boy turned he found himself surrounded by a wonderful and would-be learned activity, to which the garish theatres presented a ridiculous contrast, and the entrancing strains of music a perplexing one. Now, to the observer who sees things relatively, it must seem strange that the modern man who happens to be gifted with exceptional talent should as a child and a youth so seldom be blessed with the quality of ingenuousness and of simple individuality, that he is so little able to have these qualities at all. As a matter of fact, men of rare talent, like Goethe and Wagner, much more often attain to ingenuousness in manhood than during the more tender years of childhood and youth. And this is especially so with the artist, who, being born with a more than usual capacity for imitating, succumbs to the morbid multiformity of modern life as to a virulent disease of infancy. As a child he will more closely resemble an old man. The wonderfully accurate and original picture of youth which Wagner gives us in the Siegfried of the Nibelungen Ring could only have been conceived by a man, and by one who had discovered his youthfulness but late in life. Wagner's maturity, like his adolesence, was also late in making its appearance, and he is thus, in this respect alone, the very reverse of the precocious type.

The appearance of his moral and intellectual strength was the prelude to the drama of his soul. And how different it then became! His nature seems to have been simplified at one terrible stroke, and divided against itself into two instincts or spheres. From its innermost depths there gushes forth a passionate will which, like a rapid mountain torrent, endeavours to make its way through all paths, ravines, and crevices, in search of light and power. Only a force completely free and pure was strong enough to guide this will to all that is good and beneficial. Had it been combined with a narrow intelligence, a will with such a tyrannical and boundless desire might have become fatal; in any case, an exit into the open had to be found for it as quickly as possible, whereby it could rush into pure air and sunshine. Lofty aspirations, which continually meet with failure, ultimately turn to evil. The inadequacy of means for obtaining success may, in certain circumstances, be the result of an inexorable fate, and not necessarily of a lack of strength; but he who under such circumstances cannot abandon his aspirations, despite the inadequacy of his means, will only become embittered, and consequently irritable and intolerant. He may possibly seek the cause of his failure in other people; he may even, in a fit of passion, hold the whole world guilty; or he may turn defiantly down secret byways and secluded lanes, or resort to violence. In this way, noble natures, on their road to the most high, may turn savage. Even among those who seek but their own personal moral purity, among monks and anchorites, men are to be found who, undermined and devoured by failure, have become barbarous and hopelessly morbid. There was a spirit full of love and calm belief, full of goodness and infinite tenderness, hostile to all violence and self-deterioration, and abhorring the sight of a soul in bondage. And it was this spirit which manifested itself to Wagner. It hovered over him as a consoling angel, it covered him with its wings, and showed him the true path. At this stage we bring the other side of Wagner's nature into view: but how shall we describe this other side?

The characters an artist creates are not himself, but the succession of these characters, to which it is clear he is greatly attached, must at all events reveal something of his nature. Now try and recall Rienzi, the Flying Dutchman and Senta, Tannhauser and Elizabeth, Lohengrin and Elsa, Tristan and Marke, Hans Sachs, Woden and Brunhilda,—all these characters are correlated by a secret current of ennobling and broadening morality which flows through them and becomes ever purer and clearer as it progresses. And at this point we enter with respectful reserve into the presence of the most hidden development in Wagner's own soul. In what other artist do we meet with the like of this, in the same proportion? Schiller's characters, from the Robbers to Wallenstein and Tell, do indeed pursue an ennobling course, and likewise reveal something of their author's development; but in Wagner the standard is higher and the distance covered is much greater. In the Nibelungen Ring, for instance, where Brunhilda is awakened by Siegfried, I perceive the most moral music I have ever heard. Here Wagner attains to such a high level of sacred feeling that our mind unconsciously wanders to the glistening ice-and snow-peaks of the Alps, to find a likeness there;— so pure, isolated, inaccessible, chaste, and bathed in love-beams does Nature here display herself, that clouds and tempests—yea, and even the sublime itself—seem to lie beneath her. Now, looking down from this height upon Tannhauser and the Flying Dutchman, we begin to perceive how the man in Wagner was evolved: how restlessly and darkly he began; how tempestuously he strove to gratify his desires, to acquire power and to taste those rapturous delights from which he often fled in disgust; how he wished to throw off a yoke, to forget, to be negative, and to renounce everything. The whole torrent plunged, now into this valley, now into that, and flooded the most secluded chinks and crannies. In the night of these semi-subterranean convulsions a star appeared and glowed high above him with melancholy vehemence; as soon as he recognised it, he named it *Fidelity—unselfish fidelity*. Why did this star seem to him the brightest and purest of all? What secret meaning had the word "fidelity" to his whole being? For he has graven its image and problems upon all his thoughts and compositions. His works contain almost a complete series of the rarest and most beautiful examples of fidelity: that of brother to sister, of friend to friend, of servant to master; of Elizabeth to Tannhauser, of Senta to the Dutchman, of Elsa to Lohengrin, of Isolde, Kurvenal, and Marke to Tristan, of Brunhilda to the most secret vows of Woden—and many others. It is Wagner's most personal and most individual experience, which he reveres like a religious mystery, and which he calls Fidelity; he never wearies of breathing it into hundreds of different characters, and of endowing it with the sublimest that in him lies, so overflowing is his gratitude. It is, in short, the recognition of the fact that the two sides of his nature remained faithful to each other, that out of free and unselfish love, the creative, ingenuous, and brilliant side kept loyally abreast of the dark, the intractable, and the tyrannical side.

III.

The relation of the two constituent forces to each other, and the yielding of the one to the other, was the great requisite by which alone he could remain wholly and truly himself. At the same time, this was the only thing he could not control, and over which he could only keep a watch, while the temptations to infidelity and its threatening dangers beset him more and more. The uncertainty derived therefrom is an overflowing source of suffering for those in process of development. Each of his instincts made constant efforts to attain to unmeasured heights, and each of the capacities he possessed for enjoying life seemed to long to tear itself away from its companions in order to seek satisfaction alone; the greater their exuberance the more terrific was the tumult, and the more bitter the competition between them. In addition, accident and life fired the desire for power and splendour in him; but he was more often tormented by the cruel necessity of having to live at all, while all around him lay obstacles and snares. How is it possible for any one to remain faithful here, to be completely steadfast? This doubt often depressed him, and he expresses it, as an artist expressed his doubt, in artistic forms. Elizabeth, for instance, can only suffer, pray, and die; she saves the fickle and intemperate man by her loyalty, though not for this life. In the path of every true artist, whose lot is cast in these modern days, despair and danger are strewn. He has many means whereby he can attain to honour and might; peace and plenty persistently offer themselves to him, but only in that form recognised by the modern man, which to the straightforward artist is no better than choke-damp. In this temptation, and in the act of resisting it, lie the dangers that threaten him—dangers arising from his disgust at the means modernity offers him of acquiring pleasure and esteem, and from the indignation provoked by the selfish ease of modern society. Imagine Wagner's filling an official position, as for instance that of bandmaster at public and court theatres, both of which positions he has held: think how he, a serious artist, must have struggled in order to enforce seriousness in those very places which, to meet the demands of modern conventions, are designed with almost systematic frivolity to appeal only to the frivolous. Think how he must have partially succeeded, though only to fail on the whole. How constantly disgust must have been at his heels despite his repeated attempts to flee it, how he failed to find the haven to which he might have repaired, and how he had ever to return to the Bohemians and outlaws of our society, as one of them. If he himself broke loose from any post or position, he rarely found a better one in its stead, while more than once distress was all that his unrest brought him. Thus Wagner changed his associates, his dwelling-place and country, and when we come to comprehend the nature of the circles into which he gravitated, we can hardly realise how he was able to tolerate them for any length of time. The greater half of his past seems to be shrouded in heavy mist; for a long time he appears to have had no general hopes, but only hopes for the morrow, and thus, although he reposed no faith in the future, he was not driven to despair. He must have felt like a nocturnal traveller, broken with fatigue, exasperated from want of sleep, and tramping wearily along beneath a heavy burden, who, far from fearing the sudden approach of death, rather longs for it as something exquisitely charming. His burden, the road and the night—all would disappear! The thought was a temptation to him. Again and again, buoyed up by his temporary hopes, he plunged anew into the turmoil of life, and left all apparatus behind him. But his method of doing this, his lack of moderation in the doing, betrayed what a feeble hold his hopes had upon him; how they were only stimulants to which he had recourse in an extremity. The conflict between his aspirations and his partial or total inability to realise them, tormented him like a thorn in the flesh. Infuriated by constant privations, his imagination lapsed into the dissipated, whenever the state of want was momentarily relieved. Life grew ever more and more complicated for him; but the means and artifices that he discovered in his art as a dramatist became evermore resourceful and daring. Albeit, these were little more than palpable dramatic makeshifts and expedients, which deceived, and were invented, only for the moment. In a flash such means occurred to his mind and were used up. Examined closely and without prepossession, Wagner's life, to recall one of Schopenhauer's expressions, might be said to consist largely of comedy, not to mention burlesque. And what the artist's feelings must have been, conscious as he was, during whole periods of his life, of this undignified element in it,—he who more than any one else, perhaps, breathed freely only in sublime and more than sublime spheres,— the thinker alone can form any idea.

In the midst of this mode of life, a detailed description of which is necessary in order to inspire the amount of pity, awe, and admiration which are its due, he developed a *talent for acquiring knowledge*, which even in a German—a son of the nation learned above all others—was really extraordinary. And with this talent yet another danger threatened Wagner—a danger more formidable than that involved in a life which was apparently without either a stay or a rule, borne hither and thither by disturbing illusions. From a novice trying his strength, Wagner became a thorough master of music and of the theatre, as also a prolific inventor in the preliminary technical conditions for the execution of art. No one will any longer deny him the glory of having given us the supreme model for lofty artistic execution on a large scale. But he became more than this, and in order so to develop, he, no less than any one else in like circumstances, had to reach the highest degree of culture by virtue of his studies. And wonderfully he achieved this end! It is delightful to follow his progress. From all sides material seemed to come unto him and into him, and the larger and heavier the resulting structure became, the more rigid was the arch of the ruling and ordering thought supporting it. And yet access to the sciences and arts has seldom been made more difficult for any man than for Wagner; so much so that he had almost to break his own road through to them. The reviver of the simple drama, the discoverer of the position due to art in true human society, the poetic interpreter of bygone views of life, the philosopher, the historian, the aesthete and the critic, the master of languages, the mythologist and the myth poet, who was the first to include all these wonderful and beautiful products of primitive times in a single Ring, upon which he engraved the runic characters of his thoughts— what a wealth of knowledge must Wagner have accumulated and commanded, in order to have become all that! And yet this mass of material was just as powerless to impede the action of his will as a matter of detail—however attractive—was to draw his purpose from its path. For the exceptional character of such conduct to be appreciated fully, it should be compared with that of Goethe,— he who, as a student and as a sage, resembled nothing so much as a huge river-basin, which does not pour all its water into the sea, but spends as much of it on its way there, and at its various twists and turns, as it ultimately disgorges at its mouth. True, a nature like Goethe's not only has, but also engenders, more pleasure than any other; there is more mildness and noble profligacy in it; whereas the tenor and tempo of Wagner's power at times provoke both fear and flight. But let him fear who will, we shall only be the more courageous, in that we shall be permitted to come face to face with a hero who, in regard to modern culture, "has never learned the meaning of fear."

But neither has he learned to look for repose in history and philosophy, nor to derive those subtle influences from their study which tend to paralyse action or to soften a man unduly. Neither the creative nor the militant artist in him was ever diverted from his purpose by learning and culture. The moment his constructive powers direct him, history becomes yielding clay in his hands. His attitude towards it then differs from that of every scholar, and more nearly resembles the relation of the ancient Greek to his myths; that is to say, his subject is something he may fashion, and about which he may write verses. He will naturally do this with love and a certain becoming reverence, but with the sovereign right of the creator notwithstanding. And precisely because history is more supple and more variable than a dream to him, he can invest the most individual case with the characteristics of a whole age, and thus attain to a vividness of narrative of which historians are quite incapable. In what work of art, of any kind, has the body and soul of the Middle Ages ever been so thoroughly depicted as in Lohengrin? And will not the Meistersingers continue to acquaint men, even in the remotest ages to come, with the nature of Germany's soul? Will they not do more than acquaint men of it? Will they not represent its very ripest fruit—the fruit of that spirit which ever wishes to reform and not to overthrow, and which, despite the broad couch of comfort on which it lies, has not forgotten how to endure the noblest discomfort when a worthy and novel deed has to be accomplished?

And it is just to this kind of discomfort that Wagner always felt himself drawn by his study of history and philosophy: in them he not only found arms and coats of mail, but what he felt in their presence above all was the inspiring breath which is wafted from the graves of all great fighters, sufferers, and thinkers. Nothing distinguishes a man more from the general pattern of the age than the use he makes of history and philosophy. According to present views, the former seems to have been allotted the duty of giving modern man breathing-time, in the midst of his panting and strenuous scurry towards his goal, so that he may, for a space, imagine he has slipped his leash. What Montaigne was as an individual amid the turmoil of the Reformation—that is to say, a creature inwardly coming to peace with himself, serenely secluded in himself and taking breath, as his best reader,

Shakespeare, understood him, —this is what history is to the modern spirit today. The fact that the Germans, for a whole century, have devoted themselves more particularly to the study of history, only tends to prove that they are the stemming, retarding, and becalming force in the activity of modern society—a circumstance which some, of course, will place to their credit. On the whole, however, it is a dangerous symptom when the mind of a nation turns with preference to the study of the past. It is a sign of flagging strength, of decline and degeneration; it denotes that its people are perilously near to falling victims to the first fever that may happen to be rife —the political fever among others. Now, in the history of modern thought, our scholars are an example of this condition of weakness as opposed to all reformative and revolutionary activity. The mission they have chosen is not of the noblest; they have rather been content to secure smug happiness for their kind, and little more. Every independent and manly step leaves them halting in the background, although it by no means outstrips history. For the latter is possessed of vastly different powers, which only natures like Wagner have any notion of; but it requires to be written in a much more earnest and severe spirit, by much more vigorous students, and with much less optimism than has been the case hitherto. In fact, it requires to be treated quite differently from the way German scholars have treated it until now. In all their works there is a continual desire to embellish, to submit and to be content, while the course of events invariably seems to have their approbation. It is rather the exception for one of them to imply that he is satisfied only because things might have turned out worse; for most of them believe, almost as a matter of course, that everything has been for the best simply because it has only happened once. Were history not always a disguised Christian theodicy, were it written with more justice and fervent feeling, it would be the very last thing on earth to be made to serve the purpose it now serves, namely, that of an opiate against everything subversive and novel. And philosophy is in the same plight: all that the majority demand of it is, that it may teach them to understand approximate facts—very approximate facts—in order that they may then become adapted to them. And even its noblest exponents press its soporific and comforting powers so strongly to the fore, that all lovers of sleep and of loafing must think that their aim and the aim of philosophy are one. For my part, the most important question philosophy has to decide seems to be, how far things have acquired an unalterable stamp and form, and, once this question has been answered, I think it the duty of philosophy unhesitatingly and courageously to proceed with the task of *improving that part of the world which has been recognised as still susceptible to change.* But genuine philosophers do, as a matter of fact, teach this doctrine themselves, inasmuch as they work at endeavouring to alter the very changeable views of men, and do not keep their opinions to themselves. Genuine disciples of genuine philosophies also teach this doctrine; for, like Wagner, they understand the art of deriving a more decisive and inflexible will from their master's teaching, rather than an opiate or a sleeping draught. Wagner is most philosophical where he is most powerfully active and heroic. It was as a philosopher that he went, not only through the fire of various philosophical systems without fear, but also through the vapours of science and scholarship, while remaining ever true to his highest self. And it was this highest self which exacted *from his versatile spirit works as complete as his were,* which bade him suffer and learn, that he might accomplish such works.

IV.

The history of the development of culture since the time of the Greeks is short enough, when we take into consideration the actual ground it covers, and ignore the periods during which man stood still, went backwards, hesitated or strayed. The Hellenising of the world—and to make this possible, the Orientalising of Hellenism—that double mission of Alexander the Great, still remains the most important event: the old question whether a foreign civilisation may be transplanted is still the problem that the peoples of modern times are vainly endeavouring to solve. The rhythmic play of those two factors against each other is the force that has determined the course of history heretofore. Thus Christianity appears, for instance, as a product of Oriental antiquity, which was thought out and pursued to its ultimate conclusions by men, with almost intemperate thoroughness. As its influence began to decay, the power of Hellenic culture was revived, and we are now experiencing phenomena so strange that they would hang in the air as unsolved problems, if it were not possible, by spanning an enormous gulf of time, to show their relation to analogous phenomena in Hellenistic culture. Thus, between Kant and the Eleatics, Schopenhauer and Empedocles, Æschylus and Wagner, there is so much relationship, so many things in common, that one is vividly impressed with the very relative nature of all notions of time. It would even seem as if a whole diversity of things were really all of a piece, and that time is only a cloud which makes it hard for our eyes to perceive the oneness of them. In the history of the exact sciences we are perhaps most impressed by the close bond uniting us with the days of Alexander and ancient Greece. The pendulum of history seems merely to have swung back to that point from which it started when it plunged forth into unknown and mysterious distance. The picture represented by our own times is by no means a new one: to the student of history it must always seem as though he were merely in the presence of an old familiar face, the features of which he recognises. In our time the spirit of Greek culture is scattered broadcast. While forces of all kinds are pressing one upon the other, and the fruits of modern art and science are offering themselves as a means of exchange, the pale outline of Hellenism is beginning to dawn faintly in the distance. The earth which, up to the present, has been more than adequately Orientalised, begins to yearn once more for Hellenism. He who wishes to help her in this respect will certainly need to be gifted for speedy action and to have wings on his heels, in order to synthetise the multitudinous and still undiscovered facts of science and the many conflicting divisions of talent so as to reconnoitre and rule the whole enormous field. It is now necessary that a generation of *anti-Alexanders* should arise, endowed with the supreme strength necessary for gathering up, binding together, and joining the individual threads of the fabric, so as to prevent their being scattered to the four winds. The object is not to cut the Gordian knot of Greek culture after the manner adopted by Alexander, and then to leave its frayed ends fluttering in all directions; it is rather *to bind it after it has been loosed.* That is our task to-day. In the person of Wagner I recognise one of these anti-Alexanders: he rivets and locks together all that is isolated, weak, or in any way defective; if I may be allowed to use a medical expression, he has an *astringent power.* And in this respect he is one of the greatest civilising forces of his age. He dominates art, religion, and folklore, yet he is the reverse of a polyhistor or of a mere collecting and classifying spirit; for he constructs with the collected material, and breathes life into it, and is a *Simplifier of the Universe.* We must not be led away from this idea by comparing the general mission which his genius imposed upon him with the much narrower and more immediate one which we are at present in the habit of associating with the name of Wagner. He is expected to effect a reform in the theatre world; but even supposing he should succeed in doing this, what would then have been done towards the accomplishment of that higher, more distant mission?

But even with this lesser theatrical reform, modern man would also be altered and reformed; for everything is so intimately related in this world, that he who removes even so small a thing as a rivet from the framework shatters and destroys the whole edifice. And what we here assert, with perhaps seeming exaggeration, of Wagner's activity would hold equally good of any other genuine reform. It is quite impossible to reinstate the art of drama in its purest and highest form without effecting changes everywhere in the customs of the people, in the State, in education, and in social intercourse. When love and justice have become powerful in one department of life, namely in art, they must, in accordance with the law of their inner being, spread their influence around them, and can no more return to the stiff stillness of their former pupal condition. In order even to realise how far the attitude of the arts towards life is a sign of their decline, and how far our theatres are a disgrace to those who build and visit them, everything must be learnt over again, and that which is usual and commonplace should be regarded as something unusual and complicated. An extraordinary lack of clear judgment, a badly-concealed lust of pleasure, of entertainment at any cost, learned scruples, assumed airs of importance, and trifling with the seriousness of art on the part of those who represent it; brutality of appetite and money-grubbing on the part of promoters; the empty-mindedness and thoughtlessness of society, which only thinks of the people in so far as these serve or thwart its purpose, and which attends theatres and concerts without giving a thought to its duties,—all these things constitute the stifling and deleterious atmosphere of our modern art conditions: when, however, people like our men of culture have grown accustomed to it, they imagine that it is a condition of their healthy existence, and would immediately feel unwell if, for any reason, they were compelled to dispense with it for a while. In point of fact, there is but one speedy way of convincing oneself of the vulgarity, weirdness, and confusion of our theatrical institutions, and that is to compare them with those which once flourished in ancient Greece. If we knew nothing about the Greeks, it would perhaps be impossible to assail our present conditions at all, and objections made on the large scale conceived for the first time by Wagner would have been regarded as the dreams of people who could only be at home in outlandish places. "For men as we now find them," people would have retorted, "art of this modern kind answers the purpose and is fitting— and men have never been different." But they have been very different, and even now there are men who are far from satisfied with the existing state of affairs—the fact of Bayreuth alone demonstrates this point. Here you will find prepared and initiated spectators, and the emotion of men conscious of being at the very zenith of their happiness, who concentrate their whole being on that happiness in order to strengthen themselves for a higher and more far-reaching purpose. Here you will find the most noble self-abnegation on the part of the artist, and the finest of all spectacles —that of a triumphant creator of works which are in themselves an overflowing treasury of artistic triumphs. Does it not seem almost like a fairy tale, to be able to come face to face with such a personality? Must not they who take any part whatsoever, active or passive, in the proceedings at Bayreuth, already feel altered and rejuvenated, and ready to introduce reforms and to effect renovations in other spheres of life? Has not a haven been found for all wanderers on high and desert seas, and has not peace settled over the face of the waters? Must not he who leaves these spheres of ruling profundity and loneliness for the very differently ordered world with its plains and lower levels, cry continually like Isolde: "Oh, how could I bear it? How can I still bear it?" And should he be unable to endure his joy and his sorrow, or to keep them egotistically to himself, he will avail himself from that time forward of every opportunity of making them known to all. "Where are they who are suffering under the yoke of modern institutions?" he will inquire. "Where are my natural allies, with whom I may struggle against the ever waxing and ever more oppressive pretensions of modern erudition? For at present, at least, we have but one enemy—at present!—and it is that band of aesthetes, to whom the word Bayreuth means the completest rout—they have taken no share in the arrangements, they were rather indignant at the whole movement, or else availed themselves effectively of the deaf-ear policy, which has now become the trusty weapon of all very superior opposition. But this proves that their animosity and knavery were ineffectual in destroying Wagner's spirit or in hindering the accomplishment of his plans; it proves even more, for it betrays their weakness and the fact that all those who are at present in possession of power will not be able to withstand many more attacks. The time is at hand for those who would conquer and triumph; the vastest empires lie at their mercy, a note of interrogation hangs to the name of all present possessors of power, so far as possession may be said to exist in this respect. Thus educational institutions are said to be decaying, and everywhere individuals are to be found who have secretly deserted them. If only it were possible to invite those to open rebellion and public utterances, who even now are thoroughly dissatisfied with the state of affairs in this quarter! If only it were possible to deprive them of their faint heart and lukewarmness! I am convinced that the whole spirit of modern culture would receive its deadliest blow if the tacit support which these natures give it could in any way be cancelled. Among scholars, only those would remain loyal to the old order of things who had been infected with the political mania or who were literary hacks in any form whatever. The repulsive organisation which derives its strength from the violence and injustice upon which it relies—that is to say, from the State and Society—and which sees its advantage in making the latter ever more evil and unscrupulous,—this structure which without such support would be something feeble and effete, only needs to be despised in order to perish. He who is struggling to spread justice and love among mankind must regard this organisation as the least significant of the obstacles in his way; for he will only encounter his real opponents once he has successfully stormed and conquered modern culture, which is nothing more than their outworks.

For us, Bayreuth is the consecration of the dawn of the combat. No greater injustice could be done to us than to suppose that we are concerned with art alone, as though it were merely a means of healing or stupefying us, which we make use of in order to rid our consciousness of all the misery that still remains in our midst. In the image of this tragic art work at Bayreuth, we see, rather, the struggle of individuals against everything which seems to oppose them with invincible necessity, with power, law, tradition, conduct, and the whole order of things established. Individuals cannot choose a better life than that of holding themselves ready to sacrifice themselves and to die in their fight for love and justice. The gaze which the mysterious eye of tragedy vouchsafes us neither lulls nor paralyses. Nevertheless, it demands silence of us as long as it keeps us in view; for art does not serve the purposes of war, but is merely with us to improve our hours of respite, before and during the course of the contest,—to improve those few moments when, looking back, yet dreaming of the future, we seem to understand the symbolical, and are carried away into a refreshing reverie when fatigue overtakes us. Day and battle dawn together, the sacred shadows vanish, and Art is once more far away from us; but the comfort she dispenses is with men from the earliest hour of day, and never leaves them. Wherever he turns, the individual realises only too clearly his own shortcomings, his insufficiency and his incompetence; what courage would he have left were he not previously rendered impersonal by this consecration! The greatest of all torments harassing him, the conflicting beliefs and opinions among men, the unreliability of these beliefs and opinions, and the unequal character of men's abilities—all these things make him hanker after art. We cannot be happy so long as everything about us suffers and causes suffering; we cannot be moral so long as the course of human events is determined by violence, treachery, and injustice; we cannot even be wise, so long as the whole of mankind does not compete for wisdom, and does not lead the individual to the most sober and reasonable form of life and knowledge. How, then, would it be possible to endure this feeling of threefold insufficiency if one were not able to recognise something sublime and valuable in one's struggles, strivings, and defeats, if one did not learn from tragedy how to delight in the rhythm of the great passions, and in their victim? Art is certainly no teacher or educator of practical conduct: the artist is never in this sense an instructor or adviser; the things after which a tragic hero strives are not necessarily worth striving after. As in a dream so in art, the valuation of things only holds good while we are under its spell. What we, for the time being, regard as so worthy of effort, and what makes us sympathise with the tragic hero when he prefers death to renouncing the object of his desire, this can seldom retain the same value and energy when transferred to everyday life: that is why art is the business of the man who is recreating himself. The strife it reveals to us is a simplification of life's struggle; its problems are abbreviations of the infinitely complicated phenomena of man's actions and volitions. But from this very fact—that it is the reflection, so to speak, of a simpler world, a more rapid solution of the riddle of life—art derives its greatness and indispensability. No one who suffers from life can do without this reflection, just as no one can exist without sleep. The more difficult the science of natural laws becomes, the more fervently we yearn for the image of this simplification, if only for an instant; and the greater becomes the tension between each man's general knowledge of things and his moral and spiritual faculties. Art is with us *to prevent the bow from snapping*.

The individual must be consecrated to something impersonal—that is the aim of tragedy: he must forget the terrible anxiety which death and time tend to create in him; for at any moment of his life, at any fraction of time in the whole of his span of years, something sacred may cross his path which will amply compensate him for all his struggles and privations. This means *having a sense for the tragic.* And if all mankind must perish some day—and who could question this! —it has been given its highest aim for the future, namely, to increase and to live in such unity that it may confront its final extermination as a whole, with one spirit-with a common sense of the tragic: in this one aim all the ennobling influences of man lie locked; its complete repudiation by humanity would be the saddest blow which the soul of the philanthropist could receive. That is how I feel in the matter! There is but one hope and guarantee for the future of man, and that is *that his sense for the tragic may not die out.* If he ever completely lost it, an agonised cry, the like of which has never been heard, would have to be raised all over the world; for there is no more blessed joy than that which consists in knowing what we know—how tragic thought was born again on earth. For this joy is thoroughly impersonal and general: it is the wild rejoicing of humanity, anent the hidden relationship and progress of all that is human.

V.

Wagner concentrated upon life, past and present, the light of an intelligence strong enough to embrace the most distant regions in its rays. That is why he is a simplifier of the universe; for the simplification of the universe is only possible to him whose eye has been able to master the immensity and wildness of an apparent chaos, and to relate and unite those things which before had lain hopelessly asunder. Wagner did this by discovering a connection between two objects which seemed to exist apart from each other as though in separate spheres—that between music and life, and similarly between music and the drama. Not that he invented or was the first to create this relationship, for they must always have existed and have been noticeable to all; but, as is usually the case with a great problem, it is like a precious stone which thousands stumble over before one finally picks it up. Wagner asked himself the meaning of the fact that an art such as music should have become so very important a feature of the lives of modern men. It is not necessary to think meanly of life in order to suspect a riddle behind this question. On the contrary, when all the great forces of existence are duly considered, and struggling life is regarded as striving mightily after conscious freedom and independence of thought, only then does music seem to be a riddle in this world. Should one not answer: Music could not have been born in our time? What then does its presence amongst us signify? An accident? A single great artist might certainly be an accident, but the appearance of a whole group of them, such as the history of modern music has to show, a group only once before equalled on earth, that is to say in the time of the Greeks,—a circumstance of this sort leads one to think that perhaps necessity rather than accident is at the root of the whole phenomenon. The meaning of this necessity is the riddle which Wagner answers.

He was the first to recognise an evil which is as widespread as civilisation itself among men; language is everywhere diseased, and the burden of this terrible disease weighs heavily upon the whole of man's development. Inasmuch as language has retreated ever more and more from its true province—the expression of strong feelings, which it was once able to convey in all their simplicity—and has always had to strain after the practically impossible achievement of communicating the reverse of feeling, that is to say thought, its strength has become so exhausted by this excessive extension of its duties during the comparatively short period of modern civilisation, that it is no longer able to perform even that function which alone justifies its existence, to wit, the assisting of those who suffer, in communicating with each other concerning the sorrows of existence. Man can no longer make his misery known unto others by means of language; hence he cannot really express himself any longer. And under these conditions, which are only vaguely felt at present, language has gradually become a force in itself which with spectral arms coerces and drives humanity where it least wants to go. As soon as they would fain understand one another and unite for a common cause, the craziness of general concepts, and even of the ring of modern words, lays hold of them. The result of this inability to communicate with one another is that every product of their co-operative action bears the stamp of discord, not only because it fails to meet their real needs, but because of the very emptiness of those all-powerful words and notions already mentioned. To the misery already at hand, man thus adds the curse of convention—that is to say, the agreement between words and actions without an agreement between the feelings. Just as, during the decline of every art, a point is reached when the morbid accumulation of its means and forms attains to such tyrannical proportions that it oppresses the tender souls of artists and converts these into slaves, so now, in the period of the decline of language, men have become the slaves of words. Under this yoke no one is able to show himself as he is, or to express himself artlessly, while only few are able to preserve their individuality in their fight against a culture which thinks to manifest its success, not by the fact that it approaches definite sensations and desires with the view of educating them, but by the fact that it involves the individual in the snare of "definite notions," and teaches him to think correctly: as if there were any value in making a correctly thinking and reasoning being out of man, before one has succeeded in making him a creature that feels correctly. If now the strains of our German masters' music burst upon a mass of mankind sick to this extent, what is really the meaning of these strains? Only *correct feeling*, the enemy of all convention, of all artificial estrangement and misunderstandings between man and man: this music signifies a return to nature, and at the same time a purification and remodelling of it; for the need of such a return took shape in the souls of the most loving of men, and, *through their art, nature transformed into love makes its voice heard.*

Let us regard this as *one* of Wagner's answers to the question, What does music mean in our time? for he has a second. The relation between music and life is not merely that existing between one kind of language and another; it is, besides, the relation between the perfect world of sound and that of sight. Regarded merely as a spectacle, and compared with other and earlier manifestations of human life, the existence of modern man is characterised by indescribable indigence and exhaustion, despite the unspeakable garishness at which only the superficial observer rejoices. If one examines a little more closely the impression which this vehement and kaleidoscopic play of colours makes upon one, does not the whole seem to blaze with the shimmer and sparkle of innumerable little stones borrowed from former civilisations? Is not everything one sees merely a complex of inharmonious bombast, aped gesticulations, arrogant superficiality?—a ragged suit of motley for the naked and the shivering? A seeming dance of joy enjoined upon a sufferer? Airs of overbearing pride assumed by one who is sick to the backbone? And the whole moving with such rapidity and confusion that it is disguised and masked— sordid impotence, devouring dissension, assiduous ennui, dishonest distress! The appearance of present-day humanity is all appearance, and nothing else: in what he now represents man himself has become obscured and concealed; and the vestiges of the creative faculty in art, which still cling to such countries as France and Italy, are all concentrated upon this one task of concealing. Wherever form is still in demand in society, conversation, literary style, or the relations between governments, men have unconsciously grown to believe that it is adequately met by a kind of agreeable dissimulation, quite the reverse of genuine form conceived as a necessary relation between the proportions of a figure, having no concern whatever with the notions "agreeable" or "disagreeable," simply because it is necessary and not optional. But even where form is not openly exacted by civilised people, there is no greater evidence of this requisite relation of proportions; a striving after the agreeable dissimulation, already referred to, is on the contrary noticeable, though it is never so successful even if it be more eager than in the first instance. How far this dissimulation is *agreeable* at times, and why it must please everybody to see how modern men at least endeavour to dissemble, every one is in a position to judge, according to, the extent to which he himself may happen to be modern. "Only galley slaves know each other," says Tasso, "and if we *mistake* others, it is only out of courtesy, and with the hope that they, in their turn, should mistake us."

Now, in this world of forms and intentional misunderstandings, what purpose is served by the appearance of souls overflowing with music? They pursue the course of grand and unrestrained rhythm with noble candour—with a passion more than personal; they glow with the mighty and peaceful fire of music, which wells up to the light of day from their unexhausted depths—and all this to what purpose?

By means of these souls music gives expression to the longing that it feels for the company of its natural ally, *gymnastics*—that is to say, its necessary form in the order of visible phenomena. In its search and craving for this ally, it becomes the arbiter of the whole visible world and the world of mere lying appearance of the present day. This is Wagner's second answer to the question, What is the meaning of music in our times? "Help me," he cries to all who have ears to hear, "help me to discover that culture of which my music, as the rediscovered language of correct feeling, seems to foretell the existence. Bear in mind that the soul of music now wishes to acquire a body, that, by means of you all, it would find its way to visibleness in movements, deeds, institutions, and customs!" There are some men who understand this summons, and their number will increase; they have also understood, for the first time, what it means to found the State upon music. It is something that the ancient Hellenes not only understood but actually insisted upon; and these enlightened creatures would just as soon have sentenced the modern State to death as modern men now condemn the Church. The road to such a new though not unprecedented goal would lead to this: that we should be compelled to acknowledge where the worst faults of our educational system lie, and why it has failed hitherto to elevate us out of barbarity: in reality, it lacks the stirring and creative soul of music; its requirements and arrangements are moreover the product of a period in which the music, to which We seem to attach so much importance, had not yet been born. Our education is the most antiquated factor of our present conditions, and it is so more precisely in regard to the one new educational force by which it makes men of to-day in advance of those of bygone centuries, or by which it would make them in advance of their remote ancestors, provided only they did not persist so rashly in hurrying forward in meek response to the scourge of the moment. Through not having allowed the soul of music to lodge within them, they have no notion of gymnastics in the Greek and Wagnerian sense; and that is why their creative artists are condemned to despair, as long as they wish to dispense with music as a guide in a new world of visible phenomena. Talent may develop as much as may be desired: it either comes too late or too soon, and at all events out of season; for it is in the main superfluous and abortive, just as even the most perfect and the highest products of earlier times which serve modern artists as models are superfluous and abortive, and add not a stone to the edifice already begun. If their innermost consciousness can perceive no new forms, but only the old ones belonging to the past, they may certainly achieve something for history, but not for life; for they are already dead before having expired. He, however, who feels genuine and fruitful life in him, which at present can only be described by the one term "Music," could he allow himself to be deceived for one moment into nursing solid hopes by this something which exhausts all its energy in producing figures, forms, and styles? He stands above all such vanities, and as little expects to meet with artistic wonders outside his ideal world of sound as with great writers bred on our effete and discoloured language. Rather than lend an ear to illusive consolations, he prefers to turn his unsatisfied gaze stoically upon our modern world, and if his heart be not warm enough to feel pity, let it at least feel bitterness and hate! It were better for him to show anger and scorn than to take cover in spurious contentment or steadily to drug himself, as our "friends of art" are wont to do. But if he can do more than condemn and despise, if he is capable of loving, sympathising, and assisting in the general work of construction, he must still condemn, notwithstanding, in order to prepare the road for his willing soul. In order that music may one day exhort many men to greater piety and make them privy to her highest aims, an end must first be made to the whole of the pleasure-seeking relations which men now enjoy with such a sacred art. Behind all our artistic pastimes— theatres, museums, concerts, and the like—that aforementioned "friend of art" is to be found, and he it is who must be suppressed: the favour he now finds at the hands of the State must be changed into oppression; public opinion, which lays such particular stress upon the training of this love of art, must be routed by better judgment. Meanwhile we must reckon the *declared enemy of art* as our best and most useful ally; for the object of his animosity is precisely art as understood by the "friend of art,"—he knows of no other kind! Let him be allowed to call our "friend of art" to account for the nonsensical waste of money occasioned by the building of his theatres and public monuments, the engagement of his celebrated singers and actors, and the support of his utterly useless schools of art and picture-galleries—to say nothing of all the energy, time, and money which every family squanders in pretended "artistic interests." Neither hunger nor satiety is to be noticed here, but a dead-and-alive game is played—with the semblance of each, a game invented by the idle desire to produce an effect and to deceive others. Or, worse still, art is taken more or less seriously, and then it is itself expected to provoke a kind of hunger and craving, and to fulfil its mission in this artificially induced excitement. It is as if people were afraid of sinking beneath the weight of their loathing and dulness, and invoked every conceivable evil spirit to scare them and drive them about like wild cattle. Men hanker after pain, anger, hate, the flush of passion, sudden flight, and breathless suspense, and they appeal to the artist as the conjurer of this demoniacal host. In the spiritual economy of our cultured classes art has become a spurious or ignominious and undignified need—a nonentity or a something evil. The superior and more uncommon artist must be in the throes of a bewildering nightmare in order to be blind to all this, and like a ghost, diffidently and in a quavering voice, he goes on repeating beautiful words which he declares descend to him from higher spheres, but whose sound he can hear only very indistinctly. The artist who happens to be moulded according to the modern pattern, however, regards the dreamy gropings and hesitating speech of his nobler colleague with contempt, and leads forth the whole brawling mob of assembled passions on a leash in order to let them loose upon modern men as he may think fit. For these modern creatures wish rather to be hunted down, wounded, and torn to shreds, than to live alone with themselves in solitary calm. Alone with oneself!—this thought terrifies the modern soul; it is his one anxiety, his one ghastly fear.

When I watch the throngs that move and linger about the streets of a very populous town, and notice no other expression in their faces than one of hunted stupor, I can never help commenting to myself upon the misery of their condition. For them all, art exists only that they may be still more wretched, torpid, insensible, or even more flurried and covetous. For *incorrect feeling* governs and drills them unremittingly, and does not even give them time to become aware of their misery. Should they wish to speak, convention whispers their cue to them, and this makes them forget what they originally intended to say; should they desire to understand one another, their comprehension is maimed as though by a spell: they declare that to be their joy which in reality is but their doom, and they proceed to collaborate in wilfully bringing about their own damnation. Thus they have become transformed into perfectly and absolutely different creatures, and reduced to the state of abject slaves of incorrect feeling.

VI.

I shall only give two instances showing how utterly the sentiment of our time has been perverted, and how completely unconscious the present age is of this perversion. Formerly financiers were looked down upon with honest scorn, even though they were recognised as needful; for it was generally admitted that every society must have its viscera. Now, however, they are the ruling power in the soul of modern humanity, for they constitute the most covetous portion thereof. In former times people were warned especially against taking the day or the moment too seriously: the *nil admirari* was recommended and the care of things eternal. Now there is but one kind of seriousness left in the modern mind, and it is limited to the news brought by the newspaper and the telegraph. Improve each shining hour, turn it to some account and judge it as quickly as possible!—one would think modern men had but one virtue left—presence of mind. Unfortunately, it much more closely resembles the omnipresence of disgusting and insatiable cupidity, and spying inquisitiveness become universal. For the question is whether *mind is present at all to-day*,—but we shall leave this problem for future judges to solve; they, at least, are bound to pass modern men through a sieve. But that this age is vulgar, even we can see now, and it is so because it reveres precisely what nobler ages contemned. If, therefore, it loots all the treasures of bygone wit and wisdom, and struts about in this richest of rich garments, it only proves its sinister consciousness of its own vulgarity in so doing; for it does not don this garb for warmth, but merely in order to mystify its surroundings. The desire to dissemble and to conceal himself seems stronger than the need of protection from the cold in modern man. Thus scholars and philosophers of the age do not have recourse to Indian and Greek wisdom in order to become wise and peaceful: the only purpose of their work seems to be to earn them a fictitious reputation for learning in their own time. The naturalists endeavour to classify the animal outbreaks of violence, ruse and revenge, in the present relations between nations and individual men, as immutable laws of nature. Historians are anxiously engaged in proving that every age has its own particular right and special conditions,— with the view of preparing the groundwork of an apology for the day that is to come, when our generation will be called to judgment. The science of government, of race, of commerce, and of jurisprudence, all have that *preparatorily apologetic* character now; yea, it even seems as though the small amount of intellect which still remains active to-day, and is not used up by the great mechanism of gain and power, has as its sole task the defending—and excusing of the present

Against what accusers? one asks, surprised.

Against its own bad conscience.

And at this point we plainly discern the task assigned to modern art—that of stupefying or intoxicating, of lulling to sleep or bewildering. By hook or by crook to make conscience unconscious! To assist the modern soul over the sensation of guilt, not to lead it back to innocence! And this for the space of moments only! To defend men against themselves, that their inmost heart may be silenced, that they may turn a deaf ear to its voice! The souls of those few who really feel the utter ignominy of this mission and its terrible humiliation of art, must be filled to the brim with sorrow and pity, but also with a new and overpowering yearning. He who would fain emancipate art, and reinstall its sanctity, now desecrated, must first have freed himself from all contact with modern souls; only as an innocent being himself can he hope to discover the innocence of art, for he must be ready to perform the stupendous tasks of self-purification and self-consecration. If he succeeded, if he were ever able to address men from out his enfranchised soul and by means of his emancipated art, he would then find himself exposed to the greatest of dangers and involved in the most appalling of struggles. Man would prefer to tear him and his art to pieces, rather than acknowledge that he must die of shame in presence of them. It is just possible that the emancipation of art is the only ray of hope illuminating the future, an event intended only for a few isolated souls, while the many remain satisfied to gaze into the flickering and smoking flame of their art and can endure to do so. For they do not *want* to be enlightened, but dazzled. They rather *hate* light —more particularly when it is thrown on themselves.

That is why they evade the new messenger of light; but he follows them— the love which gave him birth compels him to follow them and to reduce them to submission. "Ye must go through my mysteries," he cries to them; "ye need to be purified and shaken by them. Dare to submit to this for your own salvation, and abandon the gloomily lighted corner of life and nature which alone seems familiar to you. I lead you into a kingdom which is also real, and when I lead you out of my cell into your daylight, ye will be able to judge which life is more real, which, in fact, is day and which night. Nature is much richer, more powerful, more blessed and more terrible below the surface; ye cannot divine this from the way in which ye live. O that ye yourselves could learn to become natural again, and then suffer yourselves to be transformed through nature, and into her, by the charm of my ardour and love!"

It is the voice *of Wagner's art* which thus appeals to men. And that we, the children of a wretched age, should be the first to hear it, shows how deserving of pity this age must be: it shows, moreover, that real music is of a piece with fate and primitive law; for it is quite impossible to attribute its presence amongst us precisely at the present time to empty and meaningless chance. Had Wagner been an accident, he would certainly have been crushed by the superior strength of the other elements in the midst of which he was placed, out in the coming of Wagner there seems to have been a necessity which both justifies it and makes it glorious. Observed from its earliest beginnings, the development of his art constitutes a most magnificent spectacle, and—even though it was attended with great suffering—reason, law, and intention mark its course throughout. Under the charm of such a spectacle the observer will be led to take pleasure even in this painful development itself, and will regard it as fortunate. He will see how everything necessarily contributes to the welfare and benefit of talent and a nature foreordained, however severe the trials may be through which it may have to pass. He will realise how every danger gives it more heart, and every triumph more prudence; how it partakes of poison and sorrow and thrives upon them. The mockery and perversity of the surrounding world only goad and spur it on the more. Should it happen to go astray, it but returns from its wanderings and exile loaded with the most precious spoil; should it chance to slumber, "it does but recoup its strength." It tempers the body itself and makes it tougher; it does not consume life, however long it lives; it rules over man like a pinioned passion, and allows him to fly just in the nick of time, when his foot has grown weary in the sand or has been lacerated by the stones on his way. It can do nought else but impart; every one must share in its work, and it is no stinted giver. When it is repulsed it is but more prodigal in its gifts; ill used by those it favours, it does but reward them with the richest treasures it possesses,—and, according to the oldest and most recent experience, its favoured ones have never been quite worthy of its gifts. That is why the nature foreordained, through which music expresses itself to this world of appearance, is one of the most mysterious things under the sun— an abyss in which strength and goodness lie united, a bridge between self and non-self. Who would undertake to name the object of its existence with any certainty?—even supposing the sort of purpose which it would be likely to have could be divined at all. But a most blessed foreboding leads one to ask whether it is possible for the grandest things to exist for the purpose of the meanest, the greatest talent for the benefit of the smallest, the loftiest virtue and holiness for the sake of the defective and faulty? Should real music make itself heard, because mankind of all creatures *least deserves to hear it, though it perhaps need it most?* If one ponder over the transcendental and wonderful character of this possibility, and turn from these considerations to look back on life, a light will then be seen to ascend, however dark and misty it may have seemed a moment before.

VII.

It is quite impossible otherwise: the observer who is confronted with a nature such as Wagner's must, willy-nilly, turn his eyes from time to time upon himself, upon his insignificance and frailty, and ask himself, What concern is this of thine? Why, pray, art thou there at all? Maybe he will find no answer to these questions, in which case he will remain estranged and confounded, face to face with his own personality. Let it then suffice him that he has experienced this feeling; let the fact *that he has felt strange and embarrassed in the presence of his own soul* be the answer to his question For it is precisely by virtue of this feeling that he shows the most powerful manifestation of life in Wagner—the very kernel of his strength—that demoniacal *magnetism* and gift of imparting oneself to others, which is peculiar to his nature, and by which it not only conveys itself to other beings, but also absorbs other beings into itself; thus attaining to its greatness by giving and by taking. As the observer is apparently subject to Wagner's exuberant and prodigally generous nature, he partakes of its strength, and thereby becomes formidable *through him and to him.* And every one who critically examines himself knows that a certain mysterious antagonism is necessary to the process of mutual study. Should his art lead us to experience all that falls to the lot of a soul engaged upon a journey, *i.e.* feeling sympathy with others and sharing their fate, and seeing the world through hundreds of different eyes, we are then able, from such a distance, and under such strange influences, to contemplate him, once we have lived his life. We then feel with the utmost certainty that in Wagner the whole visible world desires to be spiritualised, absorbed, and lost in the world of sounds. In Wagner, too, the world of sounds seeks to manifest itself as a phenomenon for the sight; it seeks, as it were, to incarnate itself. His art always leads him into two distinct directions, from the world of the play of sound to the mysterious and yet related world of visible things, and *vice versa*. He is continually forced—and the observer with him—to re-translate the visible into spiritual and primeval life, and likewise to perceive the most hidden interstices of the soul as something concrete and to lend it a visible body. This constitutes the nature of the *dithyrambic dramatist,* if the meaning given to the term includes also the actor, the poet, and the musician; a conception necessarily borrowed from Æschylus and the contemporary Greek artists—the only perfect examples of the dithyrambic dramatist before Wagner. If attempts have been made to trace the most wonderful developments to inner obstacles or deficiencies, if, for instance, in Goethe's case, poetry was merely the refuge of a foiled talent for painting; if one may speak of Schiller's dramas as of vulgar eloquence directed into uncommon channels; if Wagner himself tries to account for the development of music among the Germans by showing that, inasmuch as they are devoid of the entrancing stimulus of a natural gift for singing, they were compelled to take up instrumental music with the same profound seriousness as that with which their reformers took up Christianity,—if, on the same principle, it were sought to associate Wagner's development with an inner barrier of the same kind, it would then be necessary to recognise in him a primitive dramatic talent, which had to renounce all possibility of satisfying its needs by the quickest and most methods, and which found its salvation and its means of expression in drawing all arts to it for one great dramatic display. But then one would also have to assume that the most powerful musician, owing to his despair at having to appeal to people who were either only semi-musical or not musical at all, violently opened a road for himself to the other arts, in order to acquire that capacity for diversely communicating himself to others, by which he compelled them to understand him, by which he compelled the masses to understand him. However the development of the born dramatist may be pictured, in his ultimate expression he is a being free from all inner barriers and voids: the real, emancipated artist cannot help himself, he must think in the spirit of all the arts at once, as the mediator and intercessor between apparently separated spheres, the one who reinstalls the unity and wholeness of the artistic faculty, which cannot be divined or reasoned out, but can only be revealed by deeds themselves. But he in whose presence this deed is performed will be overcome by its gruesome and seductive charm: in a flash he will be confronted with a power which cancels both resistance and reason, and makes every detail of life appear irrational and incomprehensible. Carried away from himself, he seems to be suspended in a mysterious fiery element; he ceases to understand himself, the standard of everything has fallen from his hands; everything stereotyped and fixed begins to totter; every object seems to acquire a strange colour and to tell us its tale by means of new symbols;—one would need to be a Plato in order to discover, amid this confusion of delight and fear, how he accomplishes the feat, and to say to the dramatist: "Should a man come into our midst who possessed sufficient knowledge to simulate or imitate anything, we would honour him as something wonderful and holy; we would even anoint him and adorn his brow with a sacred diadem; but we would urge him to leave our circle for another, notwithstanding." It may be that a member of the Platonic community would have been able to chasten himself to such conduct: we, however, who live in a very different community, long for, and earnestly desire, the charmer to come to us, although we may fear him already,—and we only desire his presence in order that our society and the mischievous reason and might of which it is the incarnation may be confuted. A state of human civilisation, of human society, morality, order, and general organisation which would be able to dispense with the services of an imitative artist or mimic, is not perhaps so utterly inconceivable; but this Perhaps is probably the most daring that has ever been posited, and is equivalent to the gravest expression of doubt. The only man who ought to be at liberty to speak of such a possibility is he who could beget, and have the presentiment of, the highest phase of all that is to come, and who then, like Faust, would either be obliged to turn blind, or be permitted to become so. For we have no right to this blindness; whereas Plato, after he had cast that one glance into the ideal Hellenic, had the right to be blind to all Hellenism. For this reason, we others are in much greater need of art; because it was *in the presence of the realistic that our eyes began to see,* and we require the complete dramatist in order that he may relieve us, if only for an hour or so, of the insufferable tension arising from our knowledge of the chasm which lies between our capabilities and the duties we have to perform. With him we ascend to the highest pinnacle of feeling, and only then do we fancy we have returned to nature's unbounded freedom, to the actual realm of liberty. From this point of vantage we can see ourselves and our fellows emerge as something sublime from an immense mirage, and we see the deep meaning in our struggles, in our victories and defeats; we begin to find pleasure in the rhythm of passion and in its victim in the hero's every footfall we distinguish the hollow echo of death, and in its proximity we realise the greatest charm of life: thus transformed into tragic men, we return again to life with comfort in our souls. We are conscious of a new feeling of security, as if we had found a road leading out of the greatest dangers, excesses, and ecstasies, back to the limited and the familiar: there where our relations with our fellows seem to partake of a superior benevolence, and are at all events more noble than they were. For here, everything seemingly serious and needful, which appears to lead to a definite goal, resembles only detached fragments when compared with the path we ourselves have trodden, even in our dreams,— detached fragments of that complete and grand experience whereof we cannot even think without a thrill. Yes, we shall even fall into danger and be tempted to take life too easily, simply because in art we were in such deadly earnest concerning it, as Wagner says somewhere anent certain incidents in his own life. For if we who are but the spectators and not the creators of this display of dithyrambic dramatic art, can almost imagine a dream to be more real than the actual experiences of our wakeful hours, how much more keenly must the creator realise this contrast! There he stands amid all the clamorous appeals and importunities of the day, and of the necessities of life; in the midst of Society and State—and as what does he stand there? Maybe he is the only wakeful one, the only being really and truly conscious, among a host of confused and tormented sleepers, among a multitude of deluded and suffering people. He may even feel like a victim of chronic insomnia, and fancy himself obliged to bring his clear, sleepless, and conscious life into touch with somnambulists and ghostly well-intentioned creatures. Thus everything that others regard as commonplace strikes him as weird, and he is tempted to meet the whole phenomenon with haughty mockery. But how peculiarly this feeling is crossed, when another force happens to join his quivering pride, the craving of the heights for the depths, the affectionate yearning for earth, for happiness and for fellowship—then, when he thinks of all he misses as a hermit-creator, he feels as though he ought to descend to the earth like a god, and bear all that is weak, human, and lost, "in fiery arms up to heaven," so as to obtain love and no longer worship only, and to be able to lose himself completely in his love. But it is just this contradiction which is the miraculous fact in the soul of the dithyrambic dramatist, and if his nature can be understood at all, surely it must be here. For his creative moments in art occur when the antagonism between his feelings is at its height and when his proud astonishment and wonder at the world combine with the ardent desire to approach that same world as a lover. The glances he then bends towards the earth are always rays of sunlight which "draw up water," form mist, and gather storm-clouds. *Clear-sighted and prudent, loving and unselfish* at the same time, his glance is projected downwards; and all things that are illumined by this double ray of light, nature conjures to discharge their strength, to reveal their most hidden secret, and this through bashfulness. It is more than a mere figure of speech to say that he surprised Nature with that glance, that he caught her naked; that is why she would conceal her shame by seeming precisely the reverse. What has hitherto been invisible, the inner life, seeks its salvation in the region of the visible; what has hitherto been only visible, repairs to the dark ocean of sound: *thus Nature, in trying to conceal herself, unveils the character of her contradictions.* In a dance, wild, rhythmic and gliding, and with ecstatic movements, the born dramatist makes known something of what is going on within him, of what is taking place in nature: the dithyrambic quality of his movements speaks just as eloquently of quivering comprehension and of powerful penetration as of the approach of love and self-renunciation. Intoxicated speech follows the course of this rhythm; melody resounds coupled with speech, and in its turn melody projects its sparks into the realm of images and ideas. A dream-apparition, like and unlike the image of Nature and her wooer, hovers forward; it condenses into more human shapes; it spreads out in response to its heroically triumphant will, and to a most delicious collapse and cessation of will:—thus tragedy is born; thus life is presented with its grandest knowledge— that of tragic thought; thus, at last, the greatest charmer and benefactor among mortals—the dithyrambic dramatist—is evolved.

VIII.

Wagner's actual life—that is to say, the gradual evolution of the dithyrambic dramatist in him— was at the same time an uninterrupted struggle with himself, a struggle which never ceased until his evolution was complete. His fight with the opposing world was grim and ghastly, only because it was this same world—this alluring enemy—which he heard speaking out of his own heart, and because he nourished a violent demon in his breast—the demon of resistance. When the ruling idea of his life gained ascendancy over his mind—the idea that drama is, of all arts, the one that can exercise the greatest amount of influence over the world—it aroused the most active emotions in his whole being. It gave him no very clear or luminous decision, at first, as to what was to be done and desired in the future; for the idea then appeared merely as a form of temptation—that is to say, as the expression of his gloomy, selfish, and insatiable will, eager for *power and glory.* Influence—the greatest amount of influence—how? over whom?—these were henceforward the questions and problems which did not cease to engage his head and his heart. He wished to conquer and triumph as no other artist had ever done before, and, if possible, to reach that height of tyrannical omnipotence at one stroke for which all his instincts secretly craved. With a jealous and cautious eye, he took stock of everything successful, and examined with special care all that upon which this influence might be brought to bear. With the magic sight of the dramatist, which scans souls as easily as the most familiar book, he scrutinised the nature of the spectator and the listener, and although he was often perturbed by the discoveries he made, he very quickly found means wherewith he could enthral them. These means were ever within his reach: everything that moved him deeply he desired and could also produce; at every stage in his career he understood just as much of his predecessors as he himself was able to create, and he never doubted that he would be able to do what they had done. In this respect his nature is perhaps more presumptuous even than Goethe's, despite the fact that the latter said of himself: "I always thought I had mastered everything; and even had I been crowned king, I should have regarded the honour as thoroughly deserved." Wagner's ability. his taste and his aspirations—all of which have ever been as closely related as key to lock—grew and attained to freedom together; but there was a time when it was not so. What did he care about the feeble but noble and egotistically lonely feeling which that friend of art fosters, who, blessed with a literary and aesthetic education, takes his stand far from the common mob! But those violent spiritual tempests which are created by the crowd when under the influence of certain climactic passages of dramatic song, that sudden bewildering ecstasy of the emotions, thoroughly honest and selfless—they were but echoes of his own experiences and sensations, and filled him with glowing hope for the greatest possible power and effect. Thus he recognised *grand opera* as the means whereby he might express his ruling thoughts; towards it his passions impelled him; his eyes turned in the direction of its home. The larger portion of his life, his most daring wanderings, and his plans, studies, sojourns, and acquaintances are only to be explained by an appeal to these passions and the opposition of the outside world, which the poor, restless, passionately ingenuous German artist had to face. Another artist than he knew better how to become master of this calling, and now that it has gradually become known by means of what ingenious artifices of all kinds Meyerbeer succeeded in preparing and achieving every one of his great successes, and how scrupulously the sequence of "effects" was taken into account in the opera itself, people will begin to understand how bitterly Wagner was mortified when his eyes were opened to the tricks of the *metier* which were indispensable to a great public success. I doubt whether there has ever been another great artist in history who began his career with such extraordinary illusions and who so unsuspectingly and sincerely fell in with the most revolting form of artistic trickery. And yet the way in which he proceeded partook of greatness and was therefore extraordinarily fruitful. For when he perceived his error, despair made him understand the meaning of modern success, of the modern public, and the whole prevaricating spirit of modern art. And while becoming the critic of "effect," indications of his own purification began to quiver through him. It seems as if from that time forward the spirit of music spoke to him with an unprecedented spiritual charm. As though he had just risen from a long illness and had for the first time gone into the open, he scarcely trusted his hand and his eye, and seemed to grope along his way. Thus it was an almost delightful surprise to him to find that he was still a musician and an artist, and perhaps then only for the first time.

Every subsequent stage in Wagner's development may be distinguished thus, that the two fundamental powers of his nature drew ever more closely together: the aversion of the one to the other lessened, the higher self no longer condescended to serve its more violent and baser brother; it loved him and felt compelled to serve him. The tenderest and purest thing is ultimately—that is to say, at the highest stage of its evolution— always associated with the mightiest; the storming instincts pursue their course as before, but along different roads, in the direction of the higher self; and this in its turn descends to earth and finds its likeness in everything earthly. If it were possible, on this principle, to speak of the final aims and unravelments of that evolution, and to remain intelligible, it might also be possible to discover the graphic terms with which to describe the long interval preceding that last development; but I doubt whether the first achievement is possible at all, and do not therefore attempt the second. The limits of the interval separating the preceding and the subsequent ages will be described historically in two sentences: Wagner was the *revolutionist of society*; Wagner recognised the only artistic element that ever existed hitherto—*the poetry of the people.* The ruling idea which in a new form and mightier than it had ever been, obsessed Wagner, after he had overcome his share of despair and repentance, led him to both conclusions. Influence, the greatest possible amount of influence to be exercised by means of the stage! —but over whom? He shuddered when he thought of those whom he had, until then, sought to influence. His experience led him to realise the utterly ignoble position which art and the artist adorn; how a callous and hard-hearted community that calls itself the good, but which is really the evil, reckons art and the artist among its slavish retinue, and keeps them both in order to minister to its need of deception. Modern art is a luxury; he saw this, and understood that it must stand or fall with the luxurious society of which it forms but a part. This society had but one idea, to use its power as hard-heartedly and as craftily as possible in order to render the impotent—the people—ever more and more serviceable, base and unpopular, and to rear the modern workman out of them. It also robbed them of the greatest and purest things which their deepest needs led them to create, and through which they meekly expressed the genuine and unique art within their soul: their myths, songs, dances, and their discoveries in the department of language, in order to distil therefrom a voluptuous antidote against the fatigue and boredom of its existence— modern art. How this society came into being, how it learned to draw new strength for itself from the seemingly antagonistic spheres of power, and how, for instance, decaying Christianity allowed itself to be used, under the cover of half measures and subterfuges, as a shield against the masses and as a support of this society and its possessions, and finally how science and men of learning pliantly consented to become its drudges—all this Wagner traced through the ages, only to be convulsed with loathing at the end of his researches. Through his compassion for the people, he became a revolutionist. From that time forward he loved them and longed for them, as he longed for his art; for, alas! in them alone, in this fast disappearing, scarcely recognisable body, artificially held aloof, he now saw the only spectators and listeners worthy and fit for the power of his masterpieces, as he pictured them. Thus his thoughts concentrated themselves upon the question, How do the people come into being? How are they resuscitated?

He always found but one answer: if a large number of people were afflicted with the sorrow that afflicted him, that number would constitute the people, he said to himself. And where the same sorrow leads to the same impulses and desires, similar satisfaction would necessarily be sought, and the same pleasure found in this satisfaction. If he inquired into what it was that most consoled him and revived his spirits in his sorrow, what it was that succeeded best in counteracting his affliction, it was with joyful certainty that he discovered this force only in music and myth, the latter of which he had already recognised as the people's creation and their language of distress. It seemed to him that the origin of music must be similar, though perhaps more mysterious. In both of these elements he steeped and healed his soul; they constituted his most urgent need:—in this way he was able to ascertain how like his sorrow was to that of the people, when they came into being, and how they must arise anew if *many Wagners* are going to appear. What part did myth and music play in modern society, wherever they had not been actually sacrificed to it? They shared very much the same fate, a fact which only tends to prove their close relationship: myth had been sadly debased and usurped by idle tales and stories; completely divested of its earnest and sacred virility, it was transformed into the plaything and pleasing bauble of children and women of the afflicted people. Music had kept itself alive among the poor, the simple, and the isolated; the German musician had not succeeded in adapting himself to the luxurious traffic of the arts; he himself had become a fairy tale full Of monsters and mysteries, full of the most touching omens and auguries—a helpless questioner, something bewitched and in need of rescue. Here the artist distinctly heard the command that concerned him alone—to recast myth and make it virile, to break the spell lying over music and to make music speak: he felt his strength for drama liberated at one stroke, and the foundation of his sway established over the hitherto undiscovered province lying between myth and music. His new masterpiece, which included all the most powerful, effective, and entrancing forces that he knew, he now laid before men with this great and painfully cutting question: "Where are ye all who suffer and think as I do? Where is that number of souls that I wish to see become a people, that ye may share the same joys and comforts with me? In your joy ye will reveal your misery to me." These were his questions in Tannhauser and Lohengrin, in these operas he looked about him for his equals —the anchorite yearned for the number.

But what were his feelings withal? Nobody answered him. Nobody had understood his question. Not that everybody remained silent: on the contrary, answers were given to thousands of questions which he had never put; people gossipped about the new masterpieces as though they had only been composed for the express purpose of supplying subjects for conversation. The whole mania of aesthetic scribbling and small talk overtook the Germans like a pestilence, and ith that lack of modesty which characterises both German scholars and German journalists, people began measuring, and generally meddling with, these masterpieces, as well as with the person of the artist. Wagner tried to help the comprehension of his question by writing about it; but this only led to fresh confusion and more uproar, —for a musician who writes and thinks was, at that time, a thing unknown. The cry arose: "He is a theorist who wishes to remould art with his far-fetched notions—stone him!" Wagner was stunned: his question was not understood, his need not felt; his masterpieces seemed a message addressed only to the deaf and blind; his people— an hallucination. He staggered and vacillated. The feasibility of a complete upheaval of all things then suggested itself to him, and he no longer shrank from the thought: possibly, beyond this revolution and dissolution, there might be a chance of a new hope; on the other hand, there might not. But, in any case, would not complete annihilation be better than the wretched existing state of affairs? Not very long afterwards, he was a political exile in dire distress.

And then only, with this terrible change in his environment and in his soul, there begins that period of the great man's life over which as a golden reflection there is stretched the splendour of highest mastery. Now at last the genius of dithyrambic drama doffs its last disguise. He is isolated; the age seems empty to him; he ceases to hope; and his all-embracing glance descend once more into the deep, and finds the bottom, there he sees suffering in the nature of things, and henceforward, having become more impersonal, he accepts his portion of sorrow more calmly. The desire for great power which was but the inheritance of earlier conditions is now directed wholly into the channel of creative art; through his art he now speaks only to himself, and no longer to a public or to a people, and strives to lend this intimate conversation all the distinction and other qualities in keeping with such a mighty dialogue. During the preceding period things had been different with his art; then he had concerned himself, too, albeit with refinement and subtlety, with immediate effects: that artistic production was also meant as a question, and it ought to have called forth an immediate reply. And how often did Wagner not try to make his meaning clearer to those he questioned! In view of their inexperience in having questions put to them, he tried to meet them half way and to conform with older artistic notions and means of expression. When he feared that arguments couched in his own terms would only meet with failure, he had tried to persuade and to put his question in a language half strange to himself though familiar to his listeners. Now there was nothing to induce him to continue this indulgence: all he desired now was to come to terms with himself, to think of the nature of the world in dramatic actions, and to philosophise in music; *what desires* he still possessed turned in the direction of the *latest philosophical views*. He who is worthy of knowing what took place in him at that time or what questions were thrashed out in the darkest holy of holies in his soul—and not many are worthy of knowing all this—must hear, observe, and experience Tristan and Isolde, the real *opus metaphysicum* of all art, a work upon which rests the broken look of a dying man with his insatiable and sweet craving for the secrets of night and death, far away from life which throws a horribly spectral morning light, sharply, upon all that is evil, delusive, and sundering: moreover, a drama austere in the severity of its form, overpowering in its simple grandeur, and in harmony with the secret of which it treats—lying dead in the midst of life, being one in two. And yet there is something still more wonderful than this work, and that is the artist himself, the man who, shortly after he had accomplished it, was able to create a picture of life so full of clashing colours as the Meistersingers of Nurnberg, and who in both of these compositions seems merely to have refreshed and equipped himself for the task of completing at his ease that gigantic edifice in four parts which he had long ago planned and begun—the ultimate result of all his meditations and poetical flights for over twenty years, his Bayreuth masterpiece, the Ring of the Nibelung! He who marvels at the rapid succession of the two operas, Tristan and the Meistersingers, has failed to understand one important side of the life and nature of all great Germans: he does not know the peculiar soil out of which that essentially German gaiety, which characterised Luther, Beethoven, and Wagner, can grow, the gaiety which other nations quite fail to understand and which even seems to be missing in the Germans of to-day—that clear golden and thoroughly fermented mixture of simplicity, deeply discriminating love, observation, and roguishness which Wagner has dispensed, as the most precious of drinks, to all those who have suffered deeply through life, but who nevertheless return to it with the smile of convalescents. And, as he also turned upon the world the eyes of one reconciled, he was more filled with rage and disgust than with sorrow, and more prone to renounce the love of power than to shrink in awe from it. As he thus silently furthered his greatest work and gradually laid score upon score, something happened which caused him to stop and listen: *friends* were coming, a kind of subterranean movement of many souls approached with a message for him—it was still far from being the people that constituted this movement and which wished to bear him news, but it may have been the nucleus and first living source of a really human community which would reach perfection in some age still remote. For the present they only brought him the warrant that his great work could be entrusted to the care and charge of faithful men, men who would watch and be worthy to watch over this most magnificent of all legacies to posterity. In the love of friends his outlook began to glow with brighter colours; his noblest care—the care that his work should be accomplished and should find a refuge before the evening of his life—was not his only preoccupation. something occurred which he could only understand as a symbol: it was as much as a new comfort and a new token of happiness to him. A great German war caused him to open his eyes, and he observed that those very Germans whom he considered so thoroughly degenerate and so inferior to the high standard of real Teutonism, of which he had formed an ideal both from self-knowledge and the conscientious study of other great Germans in history; he observed that those very Germans were, in the midst of terrible circumstances, exhibiting two virtues of the highest order—simple bravery and prudence; and with his heart bounding with delight he conceived the hope that he might not be the last German, and that some day a greater power would perhaps stand by his works than that devoted yet meagre one consisting of his little band of friends—a power able to guard it during that long period preceding its future glory, as the masterpiece of this future. Perhaps it was not possible to steel this belief permanently against doubt, more particularly when it sought to rise to hopes of immediate results: suffice it that he derived a tremendous spur from his environment, which constantly reminded him of a lofty duty ever to be fulfilled.

His work would not have been complete had he handed it to the world only in the form of silent manuscript. He must make known to the world what it could not guess in regard to his productions, what was his alone to reveal— the new style for the execution and presentation of his works, so that he might set that example which nobody else could set, and thus establish *a tradition of style*, not on paper, not by means of signs, but through impressions made upon the very souls of men. This duty had become all the more pressing with him, seeing that precisely in regard to the style of their execution his other works had meanwhile succumbed to the most insufferable and absurd of fates: they were famous and admired, yet no one manifested the slightest sign of indignation when they were mishandled. For, strange to say, whereas he renounced ever more and more the hope of success among his contemporaries, owing to his all too thorough knowledge of them, and disclaimed all desire for power, both "success" and "power" came to him, or at least everybody told him so. It was in vain that he made repeated attempts to expose, with the utmost clearness, how worthless and humiliating such successes were to him: people were so unused to seeing an artist able to differentiate at all between the effects of his works that even his most solemn protests were never entirely trusted. Once he had perceived the relationship existing between our system of theatres and their success, and the men of his time, his soul ceased to be attracted by the stage at all. He had no further concern with aesthetic ecstasies and the exultation of excited crowds, and he must even have felt angry to see his art being gulped down indiscriminately by the yawning abyss of boredom and the insatiable love of distraction. How flat and pointless every effect proved under these circumstances— more especially as it was much more a case of having to minister to one quite insatiable than of cloying the hunger of a starving man— Wagner began to perceive from the following repeated experience: everybody, even the performers and promoters, regarded his art as nothing more nor less than any other kind of stage-music, and quite in keeping with the repulsive style of traditional opera; thanks to the efforts of cultivated conductors, his works were even cut and hacked about, until, after they had been bereft of all their spirit, they were held to be nearer the professional singer's plane. But when people tried to follow Wagner's instructions to the letter, they proceeded so clumsily and timidly that they were not incapable of representing the midnight riot in the second act of the Meistersingers by a group of ballet-dancers. They seemed to do all this, however, in perfectly good faith—without the smallest evil intention. Wagner's devoted efforts to show, by means of his own example, the correct and complete way of performing his works, and his attempts at training individual singers in the new style, were foiled time after time, owing only to the thoughtlessness and iron tradition that ruled all around him. Moreover, he was always induced to concern himself with that class of theatricals which he most thoroughly loathed. Had not even Goethe, m his time, once grown tired of attending the rehearsals of his Iphigenia? "I suffer unspeakably," he explained, "when I have to tumble about Wlth these spectres, which never seem to act as they should." Meanwhile Wagner's "success" in the kind of drama which he most disliked steadily increased; so much so, indeed, that the largest theatres began to subsist almost entirely upon the receipts which Wagner's art, in the guise of operas, brought into them. This growing passion on the part of the theatre-going public bewildered even some of Wagner's friends; but this man who had endured so much, had still to endure the bitterest pain of all—he had to see his friends intoxicated with his "successes" and "triumphs" everywhere where his highest ideal was openly belied and shattered. It seemed almost as though a people otherwise earnest and reflecting had decided to maintain an attitude of systematic levity only towards its most serious artist, and to make him the privileged recipient of all the vulgarity, thoughtlessness, clumsiness, and malice of which the German nature is capable. When, therefore, during the German War, a current of greater magnanimity and freedom seemed to run through every one, Wagner remembered the duty to which he had pledged himself, namely, to rescue his greatest work from those successes and affronts which were so largely due to misunderstandings, and to present it in his most personal rhythm as an example for all times. Thus he conceived *the idea of Bayreuth*. In the wake of that current of better feeling already referred to, he expected to notice an enhanced sense of duty even among those with whom he wished to entrust his most precious possession. Out of this two-fold duty, that event took shape which, like a glow of strange sunlight, will illumine the few years that lie behind and before us, and was designed to bless that distant and problematic future which to our time and to the men of our time can be little more than a riddle or a horror, but which to the fevv who are allowed to assist in its realisation is a foretaste of coming joy, a foretaste of love in a higher sphere, through which they know themselves to be blessed, blessing and fruitful, far beyond their span of years; and which to Wagner himself is but a cloud of distress, care, meditation, and grief, a fresh passionate outbreak of antagonistic elements, but all bathed in the starlight of *selfless fidelity*, and changed by this light into indescribable joy.

It scarcely need be said that it is the breath of tragedy that fills the lungs of the world. And every one whose innermost soul has a presentiment of this, every one unto whom the yoke of tragic deception concerning the aim of life, the distortion and shattering of intentions, renunciation and purification through love, are not unknown things, must be conscious of a vague reminiscence of Wagner's own heroic life, in the masterpieces with which the great man now presents us. We shall feel as though Siegfried from some place far away were relating his deeds to us: the most blissful of touching recollections are always draped in the deep mourning of waning summer, when all nature lies still in the sable twilight.

IX.

All those to whom the thought of Wagner's development as a man may have caused pain will find it both restful and healing to reflect upon what he was as an artist, and to observe how his ability and daring attained to such a high degree of independence. If art mean only the faculty of communicating to others what one has oneself experienced, and if every work of art confutes itself which does not succeed in making itself understood, then Wagner's greatness as an artist would certainly lie in the almost demoniacal power of his nature to communicate with others, to express itself in all languages at once, and to make known its most intimate and personal experience with the greatest amount of distinctness possible. His appearance in the history of art resembles nothing so much as a volcanic eruption of the united artistic faculties of Nature herself, after mankind had grown to regard the practice of a special art as a necessary rule. It is therefore a somewhat moot point whether he ought to be classified as a poet, a painter, or a musician, even using each these words in its widest sense, or whether a new word ought not to be invented in order to describe him.

Wagner's *poetic* ability is shown by his thinking in visible and actual facts, and not in ideas; that is to say, he thinks mythically, as the people have always done. No particular thought lies at the bottom of a myth, as the children of an artificial ulture would have us believe; but it is in itself a thought: it conveys an idea of the world, but through the medium of a chain of events, actions, and pains. The Ring of the Nihelung is a huge system of thought without the usual abstractness of the latter. It were perhaps possible for a philosopher to present us with its exact equivalent in pure thought, and to purge it of all pictures drawn from life, and of all living actions, in which case we should be in possession of the same thing portrayed in two completely different forms—the one for the people, and the other for the very reverse of the people; that is to say, men of theory. But Wagner makes no appeal to this last class, for the man of theory can know as little of poetry or myth as the deaf man can know of music; both of them being conscious only of movements which seem meaningless to them. It is impossible to appreciate either one of these completely different forms from the standpoint of the other: as long as the poet's spell is upon one, one thinks with him just as though one were merely a feeling, seeing, and hearing creature; the conclusions thus reached are merely the result of the association of the phenomena one sees, and are therefore not logical but actual causalities.

If, therefore, the heroes and gods of mythical dramas, as understood by Wagner, were to express themselves plainly in words, there would be a danger (inasmuch as the language of words might tend to awaken the theoretical side in us) of our finding ourselves transported from the world of myth to the world of ideas, and the result would be not only that we should fail to understand with greater ease, but that we should probably not understand at all. Wagner thus forced language back to a more primeval stage in its development a stage at which it was almost free of the abstract element, and was still poetry, imagery, and feeling; the fearlessness with which Wagner undertook this formidable mission shows how imperatively he was led by the spirit of poetry, as one who must follow whithersoever his phantom leader may direct him. Every word in these dramas ought to allow of being sung, and gods and heroes should make them their own—that was the task which Wagner set his literary faculty. Any other person in like circumstances would have given up all hope; for our language seems almost too old and decrepit to allow of one's exacting what Wagner exacted from it; and yet, when he smote the rock, he brought forth an abundant flow. Precisely owing to the fact that he loved his language and exacted a great deal from it, Wagner suffered more than any other German through its decay and enfeeblement, from its manifold losses and mutilations of form, from its unwieldy particles and clumsy construction, and from its unmusical auxiliary verbs. All these are things which have entered the language through sin and depravity. On the other hand, he was exceedingly proud to record the number of primitive and vigorous factors still extant in the current speech; and in the tonic strength of its roots he recognised quite a wonderful affinity and relation to real music, a quality which distinguished it from the highly volved and artificially rhetorical Latin languages. Wagner's poetry is eloquent of his affection for the German language, and there is a heartiness and candour in his treatment of it which are scarcely to be met with in any other German writer, save perhaps Goethe. Forcibleness of diction, daring brevity, power and variety in rhythm, a remarkable wealth of strong and striking words, simplicity in construction, an almost unique inventive faculty in regard to fluctuations of feeling and presentiment, and therewithal a perfectly pure and overflowing stream of colloquialisms—these are the qualities that have to be enumerated, and even then the greatest and most wonderful of all is omitted. Whoever reads two such poems as Tristan and the Meistersingers consecutively will be just as astonished and doubtful in regard to the language as to the music; for he will wonder how it could have been possible for a creative spirit to dominate so perfectly two worlds as different in form, colour, and arrangement, as in soul. This is the most wonderful achievement of Wagner's talent; for the ability to give every work its own linguistic stamp and to find a fresh body and a new sound for every thought is a task which only the great master can successfully accomplish. Where this rarest of all powers manifests itself, adverse criticism can be but petty and fruitless which confines itself to attacks upon certain excesses and eccentricities in the treatment, or upon the more frequent obscurities of expression and ambiguity of thought. Moreover, what seemed to electrify and scandalise those who were most bitter in their criticism was not so much the language as the spirit of the Wagnerian operas—that is to say, his whole manner of feeling and suffering. It were well to wait until these very critics have acquired another spirit themselves; they will then also speak a different tongue, and, by that time, it seems to me things will go better with the German language than they do at present.

In the first place, however, no one who studies Wagner the poet and word-painter should forget that none of his dramas were meant to be read, and that it would therefore be unjust to judge them from the same standpoint as the spoken drama. The latter plays upon the feelings by means of words and ideas, and in this respect it is under the dominion of the laws of rhetoric. But in real life passion is seldom eloquent: in spoken drama it perforce must be, in order to be able to express itself at all. When, however, the language of a people is already in a state of decay and deterioration, the word-dramatist is tempted to impart an undue proportion of new colour and form both to his medium and to his thoughts; he would elevate the language in order to make it a vehicle capable of conveying lofty feelings, and by so doing he runs the risk of becoming abstruse. By means of sublime phrases and conceits he likewise tries to invest passion with some nobility, and thereby runs yet another risk, that of appearing false and artificial. For in real life passions do not speak in sentences, and the poetical element often draws suspicion upon their genuineness when it departs too palpably from reality. Now Wagner, who was the first to detect the essential feeling in spoken drama, presents every dramatic action threefold: in a word, in a gesture, and in a sound. For, as a matter of fact, music succeeds in conveying the deepest emotions of the dramatic performers direct to the spectators, and while these see the evidence of the actors' states of soul in their bearing and movements, a third though more feeble confirmation of these states, translated into conscious will, quickly follows in the form of the spoken word. All these effects fulfil their purpose simultaneously, without disturbing one another in the least, and urge the spectator to a completely new understanding and sympathy, just as if his senses had suddenly grown more spiritual and his spirit more sensual, and as if everything which seeks an outlet in him, and which makes him thirst for knowledge, were free and joyful in exultant perception. Because every essential factor in a Wagnerian drama is conveyed to the spectator with the utmost clearness, illumined and permeated throughout by music as by an internal flame, their author can dispense with the expedients usually employed by the writer of the spoken play in order to lend light and warmth to the action. The whole of the dramatist's stock in trade could be more simple, and the architect's sense of rhythm could once more dare to manifest itself in the general proportions of the edifice; for there was no more need of "the deliberate confusion and involved variety of tyles, whereby the ordinary playwright strove in the interests of his work to produce that feeling of wonder and thrilling suspense which he ultimately enhanced to one of delighted amazement. The impression of ideal distance and height was no more to be induced by means of tricks and artifices. Language withdrew itself from the length and breadth of rhetoric into the strong confines of the speech of the feelings, and although the actor spoke much less about all he did and felt in the performance, his innermost sentiments, which the ordinary playwright had hitherto ignored for fear of being undramatic, was now able to drive the spectators to passionate sympathy, while the accompanying language of gestures could be restricted to the most delicate modulations. Now, when passions are rendered in song, they require rather more time than when conveyed by speech; music prolongs, so to speak, the duration of the feeling, from which it follows, as a rule, that the actor who is also a singer must overcome the extremely unplastic animation from which spoken drama suffers. He feels himself incited all the more to a certain nobility of bearing, because music envelopes his feelings in a purer atmosphere, and thus brings them closer to beauty.

The extraordinary tasks which Wagner set his actors and singers will provoke rivalry between them for ages to come, in the personification of each of his heroes with the greatest possible amount of clearness, perfection, and fidelity, according to that perfect incorporation already typified by the music of drama. Following this leader, the eye of the plastic artist will ultimately behold the marvels of another visible world, which, previous to him, was seen for the first time only by the creator of such works as the Ring of the Nibelung —that creator of highest rank, who, like AEschylus, points the way to a coming art. Must not jealousy awaken the greatest talent, if the plastic artist ever compares the effect of his productions with that of Wagnerian music, in which there is so much pure and sunny happiness that he who hears it feels as though all previous music had been but an alien, faltering, and constrained language; as though in the past it had been but a thing to sport with in the presence of those who were not deserving of serious treatment, or a thing with which to train and instruct those who were not even deserving of play? In the case of this earlier kind of music, the joy we always experience while listening to Wagner's compositions is ours only for a short space of time, and it would then seem as though it were overtaken by certain rare moments of forgetfulness, during which it appears to be communing with its inner self and directing its eyes upwards, like Raphael's Cecilia, away from the listeners and from all those who demand distraction, happiness, or instruction from it.

In general it may be said of Wagner the Musician, that he endowed everything in nature which hitherto had had no wish to speak with the power of speech: he refuses to admit that anything must be dumb, and, resorting to the dawn, the forest, the mist, the cliffs, the hills, the thrill of night and the moonlight, he observes a desire common to them all—they too wish to sing their own melody. If the philosopher says it is will that struggles for existence in animate and inanimate nature, the musician adds: And this will wherever it manifests itself, yearns for a melodious existence.

Before Wagner's time, music for the most part moved in narrow limits: it concerned itself with the permanent states of man, or with what the Greeks call ethos. And only with Beethoven did it begin to find the language of pathos, of passionate will, and of the dramatic occurrences in the souls of men. Formerly, what people desired was to interpret a mood, a stolid, merry, reverential, or penitential state of mind, by means of music; the object was, by means of a certain striking uniformity of treatment and the prolonged duration of this uniformity, to compel the listener to grasp the meaning of the music and to impose its mood upon him. To all such interpretations of mood or atmosphere, distinct and particular forms of treatment were necessary: others were established by convention. The question of length was left to the discretion of the musician, whose aim was not only to put the listener into a certain mood, but also to avoid rendering that mood monotonous by unduly protracting it. A further stage was reached when the interpretations of contrasted moods were made to follow one upon the other, and the charm of light and shade was discovered; and yet another step was made when the same piece of music was allowed to contain a contrast of the ethos—for instance, the contest between a male and a female theme. All these, however, are crude and primitive stages in the development of music. The fear of passion suggested the first rule, and the fear of monotony the second; all depth of feeling and any excess thereof were regarded as "unethical." Once, however, the art of the ethos had repeatedly been made to ring all the changes on the moods and situations which convention had decreed as suitable, despite the most astounding resourcefulness on the part of its masters, its powers were exhausted. Beethoven was the first to make music speak a new language—till then forbidden—the language of passion; but as his art was based upon the laws and conventions of the ETHOS, and had to attempt to justify itself in regard to them, his artistic development was beset with peculiar difficulties and obscurities. An inner dramatic factor— and every passion pursues a dramatic course—struggled to obtain a new form, but the traditional scheme of "mood music" stood in its way, and protested—almost after the manner in which morality opposes innovations and immorality. It almost seemed, therefore, as if Beethoven had set himself the contradictory task of expressing pathos in the terms of the ethos. This view does not, however, apply to Beethoven's latest and greatest works; for he really did succeed in discovering a novel method of expressing the grand and vaulting arch of passion. He merely selected certain portions of its curve; imparted these with the utmost clearness to his listeners, and then left it to them to *divine* its whole span. Viewed superficially, the new form seemed rather like an aggregation of several musical compositions, of which every one appeared to represent a sustained situation, but was in reality but a momentary stage in the dramatic course of a passion. The listener might think that he was hearing the old "mood" music over again, except that he failed to grasp the relation of the various parts to one another, and these no longer conformed with the canon of the law. Even among minor musicians, there flourished a certain contempt for the rule which enjoined harmony in the general construction of a composition and the sequence of the parts in their works still remained arbitrary. Then, owing to a misunderstanding, the discovery of the majestic treatment of passion led back to the use of the single movement with an optional setting, and the tension between the parts thus ceased completely. That is why the symphony, as Beethoven understood it, is such a wonderfully obscure production, more especially when, here and there, it makes faltering attempts at rendering Beethoven's pathos. The means ill befit the intention, and the intention is, on the whole, not sufficiently clear to the listener, because it was never really clear, even in the mind of the composer. But the very injunction that something definite must be imparted, and that this must be done as distinctly as possible, becomes ever more and more essential, the higher, more difficult, and more exacting the class of work happens to be.

That is why all Wagner's efforts were concentrated upon the one object of discovering those means which best served the purpose of *distinctness*, and to this end it was above all necessary for him to emancipate himself from all the prejudices and claims of the old "mood" music, and to give his compositions—the musical interpretations of feelings and passion—a perfectly unequivocal mode of expression. If we now turn to what he has achieved, we see that his services to music are practically equal in rank to those which that sculptor-inventor rendered to sculpture who introduced "sculpture in the round." All previous music seems stiff and uncertain when compared with Wagner's, just as though it were ashamed and did not wish to be inspected from all sides. With the most consummate skill and precision, Wagner avails himself of every degree and colour in the realm of feeling; without the slightest hesitation or fear of its escaping him, he seizes upon the most delicate, rarest, and mildest emotion, and holds it fast, as though it had hardened at his touch, despite the fact that it may seem like the frailest butterfly to every one else. His music is never vague or dreamy; everything that is allowed to speak through it, whether it be of man or of nature, has a strictly individual passion; storm and fire acquire the ruling power of a personal will in his hands. Over all the clamouring characters and the clash of their passions, over the whole torrent of contrasts, an almighty and symphonic understanding hovers with perfect serenity, and continually produces concord out of war. Taken as a whole, Wagner's music is a reflex of the world as it was understood by the great Ephesian poet—that is to say, a harmony resulting from strife, as the union of justice and enmity. I admire the ability which could describe the grand line of universal passion out of a confusion of passions which all seem to be striking out in different directions: the fact that this was a possible achievement I find demonstrated in every individual act of a Wagnerian drama, which describes the individual history of various characters side by side with a general history of the whole company. Even at the very beginning we know we are watching a host of cross currents dominated by one great violent stream; and though at first this stream moves unsteadily over hidden reefs, and the torrent seems to be torn asunder as if it were travelling towards different points, gradually we perceive the central and general movement growing stronger and more rapid, the convulsive fury of the contending waters is converted into one broad, steady, and terrible flow in the direction of an unknown goal; and suddenly, at the end, the whole flood in all its breadth plunges into the depths, rejoicing demoniacally over the abyss and all its uproar. Wagner is never more himself than when he is overwhelmed with difficulties and can exercise power on a large scale with all the joy of a lawgiver. To bring restless and contending masses into simple rhythmic movement, and to exercise one will over a bewildering host of claims and desires—these are the tasks for which he feels he was born, and in the performance of which he finds freedom. And he never loses his breath withal, nor does he ever reach his goal panting. He strove just as persistently to impose the severest laws upon himself as to lighten the burden of others in this respect. Life and art weigh heavily upon him when he cannot play wit their most difficult questions. If one considers the relation between the melody of song and that of speech, one will perceive how he sought to adopt as his natural model the pitch, strength, and tempo of the passionate man's voice in order to transform it into art; and if one further considers the task of introducing this singing passion into the general symphonic order of music, one gets some idea of the stupendous difficulties he had to overcome. In this behalf, his inventiveness in small things as in great, his omniscience and industry are such, that at the sight of one of Wagner's scores one is almost led to believe that no real work or effort had ever existed before his time. It seems almost as if he too could have said, in regard to the hardships of art, that the real virtue of the dramatist lies in self-renunciation. But he would probably have added, There is but one kind of hardship— that of the artist who is not yet free: virtue and goodness are trivial accomplishments.

Viewing him generally as an artist, and calling to mind a more famous type, we see that Wagner is not at all unlike Demosthenes: in him also we have the terrible earnestness of purpose and that strong prehensile mind which always obtains a complete grasp of a thing; in him, too, we have the hand's quick clutch and the grip as of iron. Like Demosthenes, he conceals his art or compels one to forget it by the peremptory way he calls attention to the subject he treats; and yet, like his great predecessor, he is the last and greatest of a whole line of artist-minds, and therefore has more to conceal than his forerunners: his art acts like nature, like nature recovered and restored. Unlike all previous musicians, there is nothing bombastic about him; for the former did not mind playing at times with their art, and making an exhibition of their virtuosity. One associates Wagner's art neither with interest nor with diversion, nor with Wagner himself and art in general. All one is conscious of is of the great *necessity* of it all. No one will ever be able to appreciate what severity evenness of will, and self-control the artist required during his development, in order, at his zenith, to be able to do the necessary thing joyfully and freely. Let it suffice if we can appreciate how, in some respects, his music, with a certain cruelty towards itself, determines to subserve the course of the drama, which is as unrelenting as fate, whereas in reality his art was ever thirsting for a free ramble in the open and over the wilderness.

X.

An artist who has this empire over himself subjugates all other artists, even though he may not particularly desire to do so. For him alone there lies no danger or stemming-force in those he has subjugated—his friends and his adherents; whereas the weaker natures who learn to rely on their friends pay for this reliance by forfeiting their independence. It is very wonderful to observe how carefully, throughout his life, Wagner avoided anything in the nature of heading a party, notwithstanding the fact that at the close of every phase in his career a circle of adherents formed, presumably with the view of holding him fast to his latest development He always succeeded, however, in wringing himself free from them, and never allowed himself to be bound; for not only was the ground he covered too vast for one alone to keep abreast of him with any ease, but his way was so exceptionally steep that the most devoted would have lost his breath. At almost every stage in Wagner's progress his friends would have liked to preach to him, and his enemies would fain have done so too—but for other reasons. Had the purity of his artist's nature been one degree less decided than it was, he would have attained much earlier than he actually did to the leading position in the artistic and musical world of his time. True, he has reached this now, but in a much higher sense, seeing that every performance to be witnessed in any department of art makes its obeisance, so to speak, before the judgment-stool of his genius and of his artistic temperament. He has overcome the most refractory of his contemporaries; there is not one gifted musician among them but in his innermost heart would willingly listen to him, and find Wagner's compositions more worth listening to than his own and all other musical productions taken together. Many who wish, by hook or by crook, to make their mark, even wrestle with Wagner's secret charm, and unconsciously throw in their lot with the older masters, preferring to ascribe their "independence" to Schubert or Handel rather than to Wagner. But in vain! Thanks to their very efforts in contending against the dictates of their own consciences, they become ever meaner and smaller artists; they ruin their own natures by forcing themselves to tolerate undesirable allies and friends And in spite of all these sacrifices, they still find perhaps in their dreams, that their ear turns attentively to Wagner. These adversaries are to be pitied: they imagine they lose a great deal when they lose themselves, but here they are mistaken.

Albeit it is obviously all one to Wagner whether musicians compose in his style, or whether they compose at all, he even does his utmost to dissipate the belief that a school of composers should now necessarily follow in his wake; though, in so far as he exercises a direct influence upon musicians, he does indeed try to instruct them concerning the art of grand execution. In his opinion, the evolution of art seems to have reached that stage when the honest endeavour to become an able and masterly exponent or interpreter is ever so much more worth talking about than the longing to be a creator at all costs. For, at the present stage of art, universal creating has this fatal result, that inasmuch as it encourages a much larger output, it tends to exhaust the means and artifices of genius by everyday use, and thus to reduce the real grandeur of its effect. Even that which is good in art is superfluous and detrimental when it proceeds from the imitation of what is best. Wagnerian ends and means are of one piece: to perceive this, all that is required is honesty in art matters, and it would be dishonest to adopt his means in order to apply them to other and less significant ends.

If, therefore, Wagner declines to live on amid a multitude of creative musicians, he is only the more desirous of imposing upon all men of talent the new duty of joining him in seeking the *law of style for dramatic performances*. He deeply feels the need of establishing a *traditional style* for his art, by means of which his work may continue to live from one age to another in a pure form, until it reaches that *future* which its creator ordained for it.

Wagner is impelled by an undaunted longing to make known everything relating to that foundation of a style, mentioned above, and, accordingly, everything relating to the continuance of his art. To make his work—as Schopenhauer would say— a sacred depository and the real fruit of his life, as well as the inheritance of mankind, and to store it for the benefit of a posterity better able to appreciate it,—these were *the supreme objects* of his life, and for these he bore that crown of thorns which, one day, will shoot forth leaves of bay. Like the insect which, in its last form, concentrates all its energies upon the one object of finding a safe depository for its eggs and of ensuring the future welfare of its posthumous brood,—then only to die content, so Wagner strove with equal determination to find a place of security for his works.

This subject, which took precedence of all others with him, constantly incited him to new discoveries; and these he sought ever more and more at the spring of his demoniacal gift of communicability, the more distinctly he saw himself in conflict with an age that was both perverse and unwilling to lend him its ear. Gradually however, even this same age began to mark his indefatigable efforts, to respond to his subtle advances, and to turn its ear to him. Whenever a small or a great opportunity arose, however far away, which suggested to Wagner a means wherewith to explain his thoughts, he availed himself of it: he thought his thoughts anew into every fresh set of circumstances, and would make them speak out of the most paltry bodily form. Whenever a soul only half capable of comprehending him opened itself to him, he never failed to implant his seed in it. He saw hope in things which caused the average dispassionate observer merely to shrug his shoulders; and he erred again and again, only so as to be able to carry his point against that same observer. Just as the sage, in reality, mixes with living men only for the purpose of increasing his store of knowledge, so the artist would almost seem to be unable to associate with his contemporaries at all, unless they be such as can help him towards making his work eternal. He cannot be loved otherwise than with the love of this eternity, and thus he is conscious only of one kind of hatred directed at him, the hatred which would demolish the bridges bearing his art into the future. The pupils Wagner educated for his own purpose, the individual musicians and actors whom he advised and whose ear he corrected and improved, the small and large orchestras he led, the towns which witnessed him earnestly fulfilling the duties of ws calling, the princes and ladies who half boastfully and half lovingly participated in the framing of his plans, the various European countries to which he temporarily belonged as the judge and evil conscience of their arts,—everything gradually became the echo of his thought and of his indefatigable efforts to attain to fruitfulness in the future. Although this echo often sounded so discordant as to confuse him, still the tremendous power of his voice repeatedly crying out into the world must in the end call forth reverberations, and it will soon be impossible to be deaf to him or to misunderstand him. It is this reflected sound which even now causes the art-institutions of modern men to shake: every time the breath of his spirit blew into these coverts, all that was overripe or withered fell to the ground; but the general increase of scepticism in all directions speaks more eloquently than all this trembling. Nobody any longer dares to predict where Wagner's influence may not unexpectedly break out. He is quite unable to divorce the salvation of art from any other salvation or damnation: wherever modern life conceals a danger, he, with the discriminating eye of mistrust, perceives a danger threatening art. In his imagination he pulls the edifice of modern civilisation to pieces, and allows nothing rotten, no unsound timber-work to escape: if in the process he should happen to encounter weather-tight walls or anything like solid foundations, he immediately casts about for means wherewith he can convert them into bulwarks and shelters for his art. He lives like a fugitive, whose will is not to preserve his own life, but to keep a secret— like an unhappy woman who does not wish to save her own soul, but that of the child lying in her lap: in short, he lives like Sieglinde, "for the sake of love."

For life must indeed be full of pain and shame to one who can find neither rest nor shelter in this world, and who must nevertheless appeal to it, exact things from it, contemn it, and still be unable to dispense with the thing contemned, —this really constitutes the wretchedness of the artist of the future, who, unlike the philosopher, cannot prosecute his work alone in the seclusion of a study, but who requires human souls as messengers to this future, public institutions as a guarantee of it, and, as it were, bridges between now and hereafter. His art may not, like the philosopher's, be put aboard the boat of written documents: art needs *capable men*, not letters and notes, to transmit it. Over whole periods in Wagner's life rings a murmur of distress—

his distress at not being able to meet with these capable interpreters before whom he longed to execute examples of his work, instead of being confined to written symbols; before whom he yearned to practise his art, instead of showing a pallid reflection of it to those who read books, and who, generally speaking, therefore are not artists.

In Wagner the man of letters we see the struggle of a brave fighter, whose right hand has, as it were, been lopped off, and who has continued the contest with his left. In his writings he is always the sufferer, because a temporary and insuperable destiny deprives him of his own and the correct way of conveying his thoughts—that is to say, in the form of apocalyptic and triumphant examples. His writings contain nothing canonical or severe: the canons are to be found in his works as a whole. Their literary side represents his attempts to understand the instinct which urged him to create his works and to get a glimpse of himself through them. If he succeeded in transforming his instincts into terms of knowledge, it was always with the hope that the reverse process might take place in the souls of his readers— it was with this intention that he wrote. Should it ultimately be proved that, in so doing, Wagner attempted the impossible, he would still only share the lot of all those who have meditated deeply on art; and even so he would be ahead of most of them in this, namely, that the strongest instinct for all arts harboured in him. I know of no written aesthetics that give more light than those of Wagner; all that can possibly be learnt concerning the origin of a work of art is to be found in them. He is one of the very great, who appeared amongst us a witness, and who is continually improving his testimony and making it ever clearer and freer; even when he stumbles as a scientist, sparks rise from the ground. Such tracts as "Beethoven," "Concerning the Art of Conducting," "Concerning Actors and Singers," "State and Religion," silence all contradiction, and, like sacred reliquaries, impose upon all who approach them a calm, earnest, and reverential regard. Others, more particularly the earlier ones, including "Opera and Drama," excite and agitate one; their rhythm is so uneven that, as prose they are bewildering. Their dialectics is constantly interrupted, and their course is more retarded than accelerated by outbursts of feeling; a certain reluctance on the part of the writer seems to hang over them like a pall, just as though the artist were somewhat ashamed of speculative discussions. What the reader who is only imperfectly initiated will probably find most oppressive is the general tone of authoritative dignity which is peculiar to Wagner, and which is very difficult to describe: it always strikes me as though Wagner were continually *addressing enemies*; for the style of all these tracts more resembles that of the spoken than of the written language, hence they will seem much more intelligible if heard read aloud, in the presence of his enemies, with whom he cannot be on familiar terms, and towards whom he must therefore show some reserve and aloofness, The entrancing passion of his feelings, however, constantly pierces this intentional disguise, and then the stilted and heavy periods, swollen with accessary words, vanish, and his pen dashes off sentences, and even whole pages, which belong to the best in German prose. But even admitting that while he wrote such passages he was addressing friends, and that the shadow of his enemies had been removed for a while, all the friends and enemies that Wagner, as a man of letters, has, possess one factor in common, which differentiates them fundamentally from the "people" for whom he worked as an artist. Owing to the refining and fruitless nature of their education, they are quite *devoid of the essential traits of the national character*, and he who would appeal to them must speak in a way which is not of the people—that is to say, after the manner of our best prose-writers and Wagner himself; though that he did violence to himself in writing thus is evident. But the strength of that almost maternal instinct of prudence in him, which is ready to make any sacrifice, rather tends to reinstall him among the scholars and men of learning, to whom as a creator he always longed to bid farewell. He submits to the language of culture and all the laws governing its use, though he was the first to recognise its profound insufficiency as a means of communication.

For if there is anything that distinguishes his art from every other art of modern times, it is that it no longer speaks the language of any particular caste, and refuses to admit the distinctions "literate" and "illiterate." It thus stands as a contrast to every culture of the Renaissance, which to this day still bathes us modern men in its light and shade. Inasmuch as Wagner's art bears us, from time to time, beyond itself, we are enabled to get a general view of its uniform character: we see Goethe and Leopardi as the last great stragglers of the Italian philologist-poets, Faust as the incarnation of a most unpopular problem, in the form of a man of theory thirsting for life; even Goethe's song is an imitation of the song of the people rather than a standard set before them to which they are expected to attain, and the poet knew very well how truly he spoke when he seriously assured his adherents: "My compositions cannot become popular; he who hopes and strives to make them so is mistaken."

That an art could arise which would be so clear and warm as to flood the base and the poor in spirit with its light, as well as to melt the haughtiness of the learned—such a phenomenon had to be experienced though it could not be guessed. But even in the mind of him who experiences it to-day it must upset all preconceived notions concerning education and culture; to such an one the veil will seem to have been rent in twain that conceals a future in which no highest good or highest joys exist that are not the common property of all. The odium attaching to the word "common" will then be abolished.

If presentiment venture thus into the remote future, the discerning eye of all will recognise the dreadful social insanity of our present age, and will no longer blind itself to the dangers besetting an art which seems to have roots only in the remote and distant future, and which allows its burgeoning branches to spread before our gaze when it has not yet revealed the ground from which it draws its sap. How can we protect this homeless art through the ages until that remote future is reached? How can we so dam the flood of a revolution seemingly inevitable everywhere, that the blessed prospect and guarantee of a better future—of a freer human life—shall not also be washed away with all that is destined to perish and deserves to perish?

He who asks himself this question shares Wagner's care: he will feel himself impelled with Wagner to seek those established powers that have the goodwill to protect the noblest passions of man during the period of earthquakes and upheavals. In this sense alone Wagner questions the learned through his writings, whether they intend storing his legacy to them—the precious Ring of his art—among their other treasures. And even the wonderful confidence which he reposes in the German mind and the aims of German politics seems to me to arise from the fact that he grants the people of the Reformation that strength, mildness, and bravery which is necessary in order to divert "the torrent of revolution into the tranquil river-bed of a calmly flowing stream of humanity": and I could almost believe that this and only this is what he meant to express by means of the symbol of his Imperial march.

As a rule, though, the generous impulses of the creative artist and the extent of his philanthropy are too great for his gaze to be confined within the limits of a single nation. His thoughts, like those of every good and great German, are *more than German*, and the language of his art does not appeal to particular races but to mankind in general.

But to the men of the future.

This is the belief that is proper to him; this is his torment and his distinction. No artist, of what past soever, has yet received such a remarkable portion of genius; no one, save him, has ever been obliged to mix this bitterest of ingredients with the drink of nectar to which enthusiasm helped him. It is not as one might expect, the misunderstood and mishandled artist, the fugitive of his age, who adopted this faith in self-defence: success or failure at the hands of his contemporaries was unable either to create or to destroy it Whether it glorified or reviled him, he did not belong to this generation: that was the conclusion to which his instincts led him. And the possibility of any generation's ever belonging to him is something which he who disbelieves in Wagner can never be made to admit. But even this unbeliever may at least ask, what kind of generation it will be in which Wagner will recognise his "people," and in which he will see the type of all those who suffer a common distress, and who wish to escape from it by means of an art common to them all. Schiller was certainly more hopeful and sanguine; he did not ask what a future must be like if the instinct of the artist that predicts it prove true; his command to every artist was rather—

Soar aloft in daring flight Out of sight of thine own years! In thy mirror, gleaming bright, Glimpse of distant dawn appears.

XI.

May blessed reason preserve us from ever thinking that mankind will at any time discover a final and ideal order of things, and that happiness will then and ever after beam down upon us uniformly, like the rays of the sun in the tropics. Wagner has nothing to do with such a hope; he is no Utopian. If he was unable to dispense with the belief in a future, it only meant that he observed certain properties in modern men which he did not hold to be essential to their nature, and which did not seem to him to form any necessary part of their constitution; in fact, which were changeable and transient; and that precisely *owing to these properties* art would find no home among them, and he himself had to be the precursor and prophet of another epoch. No golden age, no cloudless sky will fall to the portion of those future generations, which his instinct led him to expect, and whose approximate characteristics may be gleaned from the cryptic characters of his art, in so far as it is possible to draw conclusions concerning the nature of any pain from the kind of relief it seeks. Nor will superhuman goodness and justice stretch like an everlasting rainbow over this future land. Belike this coming generation will, on the whole, seem more evil than the present one—for in good as in evil it will be more *straightforward*. It is even possible, if its soul were ever able to speak out in full and unembarrassed tones, that it might convulse and terrify us, as though the voice of some hitherto concealed and evil spirit had suddenly cried out in our midst. Or how do the following propositions strike our ears?—That passion is better than stocism or hypocrisy; that straightforwardness, even in evil, is better than losing oneself in trying to observe traditional morality; that the free man is just as able to be good as evil, but that the unemancipated man is a disgrace to nature, and has no share in heavenly or earthly bliss; finally, that all who wish to be free must become so through themselves, and that freedom falls to nobody's lot as a gift from Heaven. However harsh and strange these propositions may sound, they are nevertheless reverberations from that future world, which *is verily in need of art*, and which expects genuine pleasure from its presence; they are the language of nature—*reinstated* even in mankind; they stand for what I have already termed correct feeling as opposed to the incorrect feeling that reigns to-day.

But real relief or salvation exists only for nature not for that which is contrary to nature or which arises out of incorrect feeling. When all that is unnatural becomes self-conscious, it desires but one thing—nonentity; the natural thing, on the other hand, yearns to be transfigured through love: the former would fain *not* be, the latter would fain be *otherwise*. Let him who has understood this recall, in the stillness of his soul, the simple themes of Wagner's art, in order to be able to ask himself whether it were nature or nature's opposite which sought by means of them to achieve the aims just described.

The desperate vagabond finds deliverance from his distress in the compassionate love of a woman who would rather die than be unfaithful to him: the theme of the Flying Dutchman. The sweet-heart, renouncing all personal happiness, owing to a divine transformation of Love into Charity, becomes a saint, and saves the soul of her loved one: the theme of Tannhauser. The sublimest and highest thing descends a suppliant among men, and will not be questioned whence it came; when, however, the fatal question is put, it sorrowfully returns to its higher life: the theme of Lohengrin. The loving soul of a wife, and the people besides, joyfully welcome the new benevolent genius, although the retainers of tradition and custom reject and revile him: the theme of the Meistersingers. Of two lovers, that do not know they are loved, who believe rather that they are deeply wounded and contemned, each demands of the other that he or she should drink a cup of deadly poison, to all intents and purposes as an expiation of the insult; in reality, however, as the result of an impulse which neither of them understands: through death they wish to escape all possibility of separation or deceit. The supposed approach of death loosens their fettered souls and allows them a short moment of thrilling happiness, just as though they had actually escaped from the present, from illusions and from life: the theme of Tristan and Isolde.

In the Ring of the Nibelung the tragic hero is a god whose heart yearns for power, and who, since he travels along all roads in search of it, finally binds himself to too many undertakings, loses his freedom, and is ultimately cursed by the curse inseparable from power. He becomes aware of his loss of freedom owing to the fact that he no longer has the means to take possession of the golden Ring—that symbol of all earthly power, and also of the greatest dangers to himself as long as it lies in the hands of his enemies. The fear of the end and the twilight of all gods overcomes him, as also the despair at being able only to await the end without opposing it. He is in need of the free and fearless man who, without his advice or assistance—even in a struggle against gods—can accomplish single-handed what is denied to the powers of a god. He fails to see him, and just as a new hope finds shape within him, he must obey the conditions to which he is bound: with his own hand he must murder the thing he most loves, and purest pity must be punished by his sorrow. Then he begins to loathe power, which bears evil and bondage in its lap; his will is broken, and he himself begins to hanker for the end that threatens him from afar off. At this juncture something happens which had long been the subject of his most ardent desire: the free and fearless man appears, he rises in opposition to everything accepted and established, his parents atone for having been united by a tie which was antagonistic to the order of nature and usage; they perish, but Siegfried survives. And at the sight of his magnificent development and bloom, the loathing leaves otan's soul, and he follows the hero's history with the eye of fatherly love and anxiety. How he forges his sword, kills the dragon, gets possession of the ring, escapes the craftiest ruse, awakens Brunhilda; how the curse abiding in the ring gradually overtakes him; how, faithful in faithfulness, he wounds the thing he most loves, out of love; becomes enveloped in the shadow and cloud of guilt, and, rising out of it more brilliantly than the sun, ultimately goes down, firing the whole heavens with his burning glow and purging the world of the curse,—all this is seen by the god whose sovereign spear was broken in the contest with the freest man, and who lost his power through him, rejoicing greatly over his own defeat: full of sympathy for the triumph and pain of his victor, his eye burning with aching joy looks back upon the last events; he has become free through love, free from himself.

And now ask yourselves, ye generation of to-day, Was all this composed *for you*? Have ye the courage to point up to the stars of the whole of this heavenly dome of beauty and goodness and to say, This is our life, that Wagner has transferred to a place beneath the stars?

Where are the men among you who are able to interpret the divine image of Wotan in the light of their own lives, and who can become ever greater while, like him, ye retreat? Who among you would renounce power, knowing and having learned that power is evil? Where are they who like Brunhilda abandon their knowledge to love, and finally rob their lives of the highest wisdom, "afflicted love, deepest sorrow, opened my eyes"? and where are the free and fearless, developing and blossoming in innocent egoism? and where are the Siegfrieds, among you?

He who questions thus and does so in vain, will find himself compelled to look around him for signs of the future; and should his eye, on reaching an unknown distance, espy just that "people" which his own generation can read out of the signs contained in Wagnerian art, he will then also understand *what Wagner will mean to this people*—something that he cannot be to all of us, namely, not the prophet of the future, as perhaps he would fain appear to us, but the interpreter and clarifier of the past.